Life, Death and After Death

LAMA YESHE

Life, Death and After Death

WITH AN INTRODUCTORY TEACHING
BY LAMA ZOPA RINPOCHE

Edited by Nicholas Ribush

LAMA YESHE WISDOM ARCHIVE • BOSTON
www.LamaYeshe.com

A non-profit charitable organization for the benefit of all
sentient beings and an affiliate of the Foundation for
the Preservation of the Mahayana Tradition
www.fpmt.org

First published 2011
10,000 copies for free distribution

LAMA YESHE WISDOM ARCHIVE
PO BOX 636
LINCOLN
MA 01773, USA

Library of Congress Cataloging-in-Publication Data
Thubten Yeshe, 1935-1984, author.
Life, Death and After Death / Thubten Yeshe ; With an Introductory
Teaching by Thubten Zopa, Rinpoche ; Edited by Nicholas Ribush.
pages cm
Includes bibliographical references.
Summary: "This book contains the last teachings Lama Yeshe gave in the
West. Poignantly, the topic was death and rebirth; six months later, Lama
Yeshe passed away. It also includes an introductory discourse by Lama Zopa
Rinpoche and concludes with a teaching on transference of consciousness
given by Lama Yeshe in London in 1982"—Provided by publisher.
ISBN 978-1-891868-25-2
1. Death—Religious aspects—Buddhism. 2. Religious life—Buddhism.
I. Thubten Zopa, Rinpoche, 1945- author. II. Ribush, Nicholas, editor. III. Title.
BQ4487.T58 2011, 294.3'423—dc22
2010050521
ISBN 978-1-891868-25-2

10 9 8 7 6 5 4 3 2 1

Cover photograph by Ueli Minder • Cover line art by Robert Beer
Interior photographs, Geneva 1983, by Ueli Minder
Designed by Gopa & Ted2 Inc.

♻ Printed in the USA with environmental mindfulness on 30% PCW
recycled paper. The following resources have been saved: 15 trees,
410 lbs. of solid waste, 6,753 gallons of water, 1,402 lbs.
of greenhouse gases and 5 million BTUs of energy.

Please contact the LAMA YESHE WISDOM ARCHIVE
for more copies of this and our other free books

···Contents···

··· Publisher's Acknowledgments ···

WE ARE EXTREMELY GRATEFUL to our friends and supporters who have made it possible for the LAMA YESHE WIS-
DOM ARCHIVE to both exist and function: to Lama Yeshe and Lama
Zopa Rinpoche, whose kindness is impossible to repay; to Peter and
Nicole Kedge and Venerable Ailsa Cameron for their initial work
on the ARCHIVE; to Venerable Roger Kunsang, Lama Zopa's tire-
less assistant, for his kindness and consideration; and to our sustain-
ing supporters: Barry and Connie Hershey, Joan Halsall, Tony Steel,
Vajrayana Institute, Claire Atkins, Thubten Yeshe, Roger and Claire
Ash-Wheeler, Hawk Furman, Richard Gere, Lily Chang Wu, Doss
McDavid, Therese Miller, Janet Hintermann, Tom and Suzanne Cas-
tles, Doren and Mary Harper and other anonymous benefactors.

In particular, we thank the late, great Henry Lau and Catherine
Lau, Wee Sin Tho and Wee Geok Hua for sponsoring the editing
and production of this book and the DVD of these teachings.

We are also deeply grateful to all those who have become members of the ARCHIVE over the past few years. Details of our membership program may be found at the back of this book, and if you are
not a member, please do consider joining up. Due to the kindness
of those who have, we now have several editors working on our
vast collection of teachings for the benefit of all. We have posted

our list of individual and corporate members on our website, www. LamaYeshe.com.

Furthermore, we would like to express our appreciation for the kindness and compassion of all those other generous benefactors who have contributed funds to our work since we began publishing free books. Thankfully, you are too numerous to mention individually in this book, but we value highly each and every donation made to spreading the Dharma for the sake of the kind mother sentient beings and now pay tribute to you all on our website. Thank you so much.

Finally, I would like to thank the many other kind people who have asked that their donations be kept anonymous; my wife, Wendy Cook, for her constant help and support; our dedicated office staff, Jennifer Barlow and Ven. Ani Tenzin Desal; Ven. Ailsa Cameron for her decades of meticulous editing; Ven. Connie Miller, Gordon McDougall, Michelle Bernard and our other editors; Ven. Kunsang for his tireless work recording Lama Zopa Rinpoche; Ven. Thubten Labdron, Ven. Thubten Munsel and Dr. Su Hung for their help with transcribing; Sandy Smith and our team of volunteer web editors; Ven. Bob Alcorn for his incredible work on our Lama Yeshe DVDs; David Zinn for his digital imaging expertise; Jonathan Steyn for his help with our audio work; Mandala Books and Wisdom Books for their help with our distribution in Australia and Europe and Amitabha Buddhist Centre and Losang Dragpa Centre for their help with our distribution in Singapore and Malaysia respectively; and everybody else who helps us in so many ways. Thank you all.

If you, dear reader, would like to join this noble group of open-hearted altruists by contributing to the production of more books by Lama Yeshe or Lama Zopa Rinpoche or to any other aspect of the Lama Yeshe Wisdom Archive's work, please contact us to find out how.

—*Dr. Nicholas Ribush*

*Through the merit of having contributed to the spread of the Buddha's
teachings for the sake of all sentient beings, may our benefactors
and their families and friends have long and healthy lives,
all happiness, and may all their Dharma
wishes be instantly fulfilled.*

· · · · ·

··· Editor's Preface ···

F OR LAMA YESHE, 1983 was a typically busy year of travel and teaching. Tragically, it was also his last. Italy, Spain, Italy again, India, America, France, Sweden, back to Italy, Switzerland, and finally, India and Nepal. The teachings in this book were Lama's last in the West; poignantly, a weekend seminar on death in Geneva.

For years, Lama had been telling us he would die soon, but he didn't, and his seemingly boundless energy and joie de vivre in the face of his serious heart disease and the unthinkability of his no longer being around lulled most of us into a state of denial. So when he would say things like his final words at this seminar, "you can write me; I'm not going to disappear immediately," those were the statements we liked to rely on. Well, five months later Lama gave us his most direct teaching on impermanence when he did disappear once and for all. But at least he lives on in his books, audio and video, and we at the LYWA are doing our best to preserve Lama's wisdom and make it available to all.

The organizers of the Geneva seminar videoed the event and we have issued this footage on a DVD also entitled *Life, Death and After Death*. And as we had a video of Lama teaching on transference of consciousness at the time of death in London the previous year, we have included that in this book and on the DVD as well. Lama Zopa

Rinpoche gave a general talk during the Geneva seminar; we open the book with that.

Hence this book has three parts: Rinpoche's introductory lecture, Lama's teaching on the death process, and Lama's 1982 talk on transference of consciousness.

I would like to thank Wendy Cook and Jennifer Barlow for their kind editorial suggestions. We hope you enjoy this free book and will also get the DVD to derive even more benefit from these teachings.

Introductory Teaching
Finding Peace in Everyday Life

LAMA ZOPA RINPOCHE

Geneva 1983

··· 1 ···
Finding Peace in Everyday Life

T HE HAPPINESS we desire, the suffering we do not want, the happiness we try to get, the suffering we try to eliminate all come from the mind—not from somebody else's mind but from our own.

For example, how does the everyday, unwanted suffering that we try to prevent come from our own mind? It arises because our mind is not under our control; we're under the control of our mind, which in turn is under the control of our disturbing thoughts. This is the mistake we make. We allow our mind to be controlled by the inner enemy; we offer the victory to the disturbing thoughts, we always give liberation to the disturbing thoughts—ignorance, dissatisfaction, anger and selfishness. Instead of defeating and trying to get freedom from them we give them complete freedom and take defeat upon ourselves. That's the whole problem. That's it. That's our everyday life.

If we make an effort to put our disturbing thoughts under the control of our mind, we'll find happiness and peace in our everyday life and our unwanted suffering will cease. But as long as we allow ourselves to be controlled by our disturbing thoughts, we'll always experience problems and suffering.

If we want peace of mind in our everyday life, then even if we can't renounce ourself and completely single-pointedly cherish other sentient beings, if we can't change that much, at least we should practice equanimity, understanding that we and other sentient beings are exactly equal in not desiring even the slightest discomfort and not being happy and satisfied. In this, we're exactly equal.

The tantric teaching, *Guru Puja,* explains that simply knowing or understanding the words of the teachings is not enough—the purpose of the words is that they be put into practice. If we don't practice what we know, we will not experience peace of mind. So here, if we can't practice exchanging ourself for others—renouncing ourself and completely cherishing other sentient beings—we should at least try to practice equanimity.

Equanimity

It's very logical. If you check carefully, you will see that you yourself, your family, friends and workmates, everybody in the country and indeed all sentient beings are all exactly equal in wanting happiness and not wanting suffering. Therefore there's not the slightest reason that your own happiness and freedom from suffering are more important than anybody else's.

First, think of your spouse and somebody you hate, your enemy: they're exactly equal. You can't find a single reason to prove that the freedom from suffering and happiness of the person you love are more important than those of the person who disturbs you. Then think in the same way about the rest of your family, your workmates, the people in your society, your country, the whole earth, and then all the other sentient beings. They're all exactly equal, even though they speak different languages, dress differently and have different colored skins. However different they are, they're exactly the same in this.

So you and the person who disturbs you, your enemy, are exactly equal in longing for happiness and not desiring the slightest discomfort and not wanting to hear even two unpleasant words. Furthermore, you and any other person are also exactly equal in having the right to obtain happiness and eliminate suffering. You and others are also exactly the same in that you need others' help and they need yours. So if, while this is the actual situation, you give harm to others for no valid reason other than you want happiness for yourself and don't care about that of others, that's very upsetting, most ungenerous; such a person has a very poor mind, a most upsetting character.

On the other hand, if, in a family, or even a couple, at least one person practices equanimity, there'll be much peace and harmony in that relationship.

Actually, the equality I've been talking about is a fact, but our wrong conception fabricates that "I'm more important than others, than my enemy, than all sentient beings," even though there's not the slightest shred of evidence for that. In fact, the I that is more important than others does not even exist; it's a hallucination. So clinging to a hallucination is rather funny, but it's what we do all the time in our everyday life. And from that, all confusion arises.

The faults of self-cherishing

This selfish attitude is the source of all our depression, aggression, nervous breakdowns, lack of success, encountering undesirable things, life's ups and downs and everyday problems. The stronger our selfish attitude, the greater the problems we experience, and the stronger our self-concern, our desire for self-happiness, the easier we find discomfort. We even get angry at birds chirping outside our window. Even though they have no intention of disturbing us and other people find their sound charming, their singing becomes a big disturbance for selfish people like us. We get angry at dogs barking and even the wind in the trees! If we're served cooked food that's even a little bit cold, we make it a huge problem. Many upsetting things like this happen. For other people, the many things that bother the selfish person are never a problem.

So you can see from just these few examples, it all comes from the selfish person's mind. If he goes into town, he gets disturbed; if he stays at home, he gets disturbed. Wherever he goes he gets disturbed.

And you see this especially with selfish couples—they fight all the time. They fight in the garden, they fight inside; in the bedroom, the dining room, at breakfast and at lunch. The only time they don't fight is when they're apart. What we see others going through and what we experience ourselves is exactly what the Buddha explained in his teachings.

But if at least one of the two renounces his or her own happiness in favor of the other's, their relationship becomes peaceful and harmonious—the greater the renunciation, the greater the peace and harmony.

So simply from this you can understand how incredibly important it is to change the mind, to practice equanimity, to develop the mind—to change the old mind, which cherishes only oneself, to the mind that cherishes others. Even for everyday peace, leaving aside the question of ultimate happiness, it's extremely important to practice the good heart.

If we always allow our mind to remain under the control of the selfish attitude, if we don't make some change in our mind, even if we were to live a billion eons, it wouldn't matter: we wouldn't have any peace of mind, we'd always experience problems. The longer we lived, the more problems we'd experience. That's what would happen. And even if out of dissatisfaction we were to change husbands, wives, companions a million times, we'd still not be satisfied; we'd still not find peace of mind.

You can see how logical and fact-based this is. It's so clear. For example, if you and another person are starving and the other person finds some food and offers it to you, giving up his happiness for yours, how happy it makes you. That shows how abandoning self-cherishing causes happiness.

If other people treat you badly, criticize you and point out your mistakes and it hurts your mind, that itself is a shortcoming of the selfish attitude. If you weren't clinging to yourself, cherishing yourself, whatever bad things other people said about you won't hurt you. Criticism hurts only if you cherish yourself.

In order to defeat and destroy the selfish attitude you have to see it as an enemy, just as you identify certain other beings as external enemies. In order to see self-cherishing as an enemy you have to be constantly aware of its shortcomings. For example, if you're trying to practice Dharma but whatever you do with your body, speech and mind does not become Dharma, that's the fault of the selfish attitude; your actions do not become Dharma because you're following the selfish attitude.

Even though we receive all kinds of thought training teachings from many different lamas, when we encounter problems we can't even remember the teachings we've received let alone put them into practice. When somebody treats us badly or abuses us, we can't even remember what meditation we should practice at that time. Why is that? It's because we're following the selfish attitude. As long as we do this, even if the buddhas of the three times were to come before us and give us teachings for a hundred eons, as long as we haven't changed our attitude, as long as we haven't practiced the instructions we've received, those buddhas' teachings would be of no benefit; they would not change our mind. If we don't make an effort from our side, no matter who gives us teachings, even Jesus himself, nothing happens; there's no peace of mind.

Even though we think we're practicing Dharma and have taken the various levels of vow—pratimoksha, bodhisattva and tantric— we can point to none of our vows as clean, pure. Our vows are like rags riddled with holes. Our pratimoksha vows are full of holes; our bodhisattva vows are full of holes; our tantric vows are full of holes. All this is because we insist on following the selfish attitude. As long as we do so, even our wishes for our own happiness don't get fulfilled; the actions we do for our own benefit do not succeed.

Not only does selfishness prevent our accomplishing activities done for ourself and experiencing temporary happiness, it also prevents us from ceasing all our obscurations and experiencing ultimate happiness. And the selfish attitude also prevents us from completing perfect activities for others, from completing the realizations that lead to the omniscient mind. In other words, simply harboring the selfish attitude itself is harming all other sentient beings.

If you think about it properly you will see that one's selfishness definitely harms all sentient beings. Without completing the realizations, we cannot work properly for others, we cannot guide every sentient being perfectly; we cannot free them from suffering and lead them into the peerless happiness of enlightenment. Therefore, simply harboring the selfish attitude itself greatly harms our ability to fulfill our work for other sentient beings. This is very clear.

You can see how incredibly important it is to understand how this works, even for those who don't understand or have faith in reincarnation. To experience even everyday happiness we have to overcome self-cherishing. Everything we've done throughout our entire life has been to achieve happiness. As children we went to primary and secondary school; as young adults we went to college; we learned many different languages, studied many different topics— what was it all for? It was to make our life happy, that's all. That's clear; it's very simple. We've put so much effort into this, for thirty or forty years, to accumulate wealth, enjoy a good reputation and so forth. We've even risked our life for happiness. So you can see how incredibly important it is to understand what actually brings happiness.

The answer: practicing patience

Therefore, the first thing we have to do in our everyday life is to change our attitude and, when we have an enemy, practice patience with that person. When somebody disturbs us we have to take that opportunity to practice patience. We have to generate equanimity, renouncing ourself and cherishing others, by thinking of the kindness of others and the shortcomings of self-cherishing. At the very least we have to practice equanimity. So you can see that developing a good heart is the very first thing we need to do.

No matter how much wealth and material we have accumulated, no matter how many decades we've studied, no matter how good our reputation, no matter how many people we have below us, working for us, if we don't practice patience and the good heart we'll have no peace of mind at all. Even if we have spent millions of dollars on houses all over the world, as long as we haven't dealt with the self-cherishing mind we'll have no peace of mind.

Where does peace of mind actually come from? It comes from the enemy. In practice, the person who disturbs us is the one who offers us peace of mind. By practicing patience and generating loving kindness and compassion for this person, our anger diminishes. Year by year we find it harder and harder to get angry, and when we do it lasts for shorter and shorter periods of time. Friends and helpers don't give us the opportunity to practice patience, loving kindness and compassion. We have to rely on enemies for that.

So you can see now, after spending up to fifty years in search of a happy life and peace of mind, spending millions of dollars obtaining a good education and buying things, if we don't practice patience and the good heart and try to change our mind, we'll have no peace at all. All our problems will remain the same if not worse...worse than the ones we had before we were educated, when we were children. This is our experience; we can see this even now.

But if right now we practice patience, loving kindness and compassion with our enemy, the person who disturbs and criticizes us in everyday life, we'll develop great realizations and incredible tranquility of mind. So you can see, whatever peace of mind you're experiencing this minute, this hour, has come from your enemy. If that person hadn't had thoughts of dislike toward you, anger for you, if he hadn't wanted to harm you, you wouldn't have had the opportunity to practice patience and therefore wouldn't have the mental peace and tranquility that you do. Your peace of mind comes from that person. Therefore, the person who is angry with you, who dislikes and wants to harm you is incredibly precious and kind.

As I just mentioned, some years ago, before you practiced patience, whenever you were angry with somebody, it would last for weeks and months. Just seeing a photo of that person or even remembering him would be painful. But after years of practice, when anger does arise it lasts for only a few seconds, then disappears. Your mind definitely changes. Before practicing thought training, you saw the person who disturbed and criticized you as very ugly, very undesirable, completely negative and painful, but now you see that angry, critical person as extremely precious and kind. You see that person in a warm aspect, like your mother, somebody who has helped you and been very kind to you. Actually, you feel even warmer toward your enemy than you do toward your mother.

So now you can see, as soon as you practice patience with your enemy, you immediately get the peace of mind that you didn't get by studying and spending lots of money for many years; the moment you practice patience, you get the peace of mind you didn't get from your vast collection of material possessions. So you can see how incredibly precious and important it is to practice the good heart…and it doesn't cost a dime.

As it says in the Kadampa teaching, *Eight Verses of Thought Transformation*, by seeing your enemy, the person who is angry with you, as your guru, your virtuous friend who helps you complete the practice of the perfection of patience, you are able to eradicate all obscurations and complete all realizations and achieve the state of omniscience.[1] Then, with no effort at all, you are able to guide all sentient beings without the slightest mistake.

So all these advantages—achieving the omniscient mind, guiding each and every sentient being to freedom from suffering and peerless happiness without mistake—derive from your enemy, from the sentient being who is angry with you. Therefore this being is incredibly precious.

If you don't practice patience with your enemy you get hell; if you do, you get enlightened.

Even if somebody were to give you a billion dollars, or every diamond on earth, you still couldn't buy the tranquility and peace of mind that you get by practicing loving kindness, compassion and patience with the sentient being who is angry with you.

---

[1] Verse 6: "When someone whom I have benefited and in whom I have great hopes gives me terrible harm, I shall regard that person as my holy guru."

So, you see, even without talking about enlightenment or all the other ultimate benefits you get from the enemy, just talking about the diminishing anger and everyday peace of mind you receive, if you were to offer your enemy the whole earth filled with jewels every hour of every day for a hundred eons, that would be nothing compared to the benefit you get from practicing patience on him. Even giving him that many jewels can never repay his kindness in offering you the chance to practice patience and the advantages, the great peace of mind, you get from that.

When we look around we see living beings everywhere—in the sky, in the water, in the bushes—all keeping busy in a never-ending quest for happiness. All those people keeping busy in cities, in villages, in space, under water, it's all for happiness. But you now understand that the first thing to ensure that such quests are successful is to practice patience in everyday life, the thought of living kindness and compassion, bodhicitta. That's the first thing to be concerned about, the most important thing.

And you also understand that to find peace of mind, to practice patience, you don't have to travel the world, you don't have to spend a lot of money, looking for an enemy, trying to find an enemy. Enemies are everywhere! Right there in your family, for example. You don't have go to the tourist office: "Please, can you direct me to an enemy? I have to practice patience." Enemies are all around you, every day—in your home, in your office, on the street. Right there. They're so kind. You don't have to spend millions of dollars to find them in order to practice patience, to find peace of mind, to develop a good heart. They're so kind; they come to you. It's like accidentally finding a million dollars in the garbage, like finding a precious treasure right in front of you without having to seek afar.

Also, that person isn't your enemy all the time. If he were, if he were constantly angry with you, every day, month and year, you'd be incredibly fortunate because you'd be able to practice patience all the time, every day, year after year. But it's not like that—sometimes he's not angry with you and there's no opportunity to practice. So if you don't take the opportunity to practice when he's mad at you, you lose that great chance of developing your mind, a good heart.

So without delay, we should practice the moment that that precious treasure found without effort—the angry person—appears before us. That should be our plan. Otherwise, even though we receive many teachings on patience and thought training, years go by without practice. Then one day, all of a sudden, we die, and that's it. Our life is over and we never practiced.

Thus you can see how rare, kind and precious are those who are angry with us. We should always remember their kindness and never miss the opportunity of practicing patience when they give it to us, as difficult as that may be. In fact, this should be our heart practice. It's easy to practice with other sentient beings; we should make our heart practice that which is the most difficult. If we can remember the kindness of the enemy and practice patience and develop bodhicitta with him, we'll find it easy to practice with other sentient beings.

In this way, then, wherever you are—at home with your parents and family or living alone—you're happy, you always enjoy your life. If you practice the good heart—renouncing yourself and cherishing others—you're happy wherever you live. If you live in the city, you're happy; if you live in the mountains, you're happy there as well. When you go to work in your office there's nobody there to whom you have to show an angry face or feel uptight with. Wherever you go, much happiness surrounds you. Not only are you happy but you also make the people you meet happy. Others are always happy to see you and want to meet you. Even if you don't particularly want a good reputation, because of your good heart you automatically get one. Even if you don't need help, others want to help you. Your life is happy and your future lives are even happier.

So when you go to work, remember the kindness of others every day. This is extremely important. You should at least remember the kindness of your employer, the person who gives you your job. Even though you get paid for your work you should still have the right attitude of gratitude. Everyday life problems come from not having the right attitude. Thinking in the wrong way brings problems; thinking in the right way brings much peace and harmony. It all depends on attitude. So when you go to work in the morning you should go with the attitude remembering the kindness of those who give you your job. Your being able to afford all life's necessities, comforts and pleasures is due to their kindness. Because of this you are also able to practice Dharma and develop a good heart.

Therefore, remembering your employers' kindness, go to work in order to alleviate their suffering and bring them happiness. If you can't manage to think of all sentient beings you should at least remember your employers. Instead of thinking, "I'm going to work for my own happiness, for my food, for my comfort," go with the attitude that you're working for others.

Similarly, whenever you eat, drink, go to bed or do anything else enjoyable, do it for the sake of other sentient beings. Think, "The purpose of my having been born human is to eliminate the suffering of other sentient beings and to bring them happiness. The purpose of my human life is to serve others, to use myself for others. Therefore I'm going to eat this food…wear these clothes…go to sleep." Do whatever you do as the servant of other sentient beings.

As the great bodhisattva Khunu Lama Tenzin Gyaltsen, His Holiness the Dalai Lama's guru, said, "If you look, look with bodhicitta; if you eat, eat with bodhicitta; if you speak, speak with bodhicitta; if you examine, examine with bodhicitta." Whatever you do, as much as possible do it with the thought of benefiting others.

One more thing: when you see somebody who's angry with you, remember that that person has no freedom at all. He's completely overwhelmed by anger, like a crazy person under the control of drugs or spirits. He has no freedom at all; he's completely possessed by anger. Think how pitiful he is and generate the thought of compassion. If you think about the situation carefully you will see that his lack of freedom itself is reason enough to generate compassion.

I'll stop here, but I hope that you've found something beneficial in what I've said; something useful that you can apply in your everyday life to find peace of mind. Thank you very much.

Life, Death and After Death

LAMA YESHE

Geneva, 1983

··· 2 ···
Why We Should Understand
the Death Process[2]

TONIGHT I'M GOING to give a brief introduction to the Buddhist view of human reality, focusing on death, the intermediate state and so forth.

Buddhism explains human beings' higher qualities of intuition, intellect and intelligence; we maintain that human growth is very different from that of vegetables. Each of us has a long history; we've been developing a long time, especially our consciousness.

Buddhism also explains that the fundamental nature of human consciousness is pure and clear; that the nuclear essence of human beings is their mind, not this body of flesh and blood. Furthermore, we believe that recognizing our lives as pleasurable or miserable depends largely on how our mind interprets them. If you *think* your life is miserable, it *becomes* miserable.

Therefore, at their root, human problems are created by each individual's mind, not by God or Buddha. But since we have the ability to mess up our own lives, we also have the ability to solve our own problems.

---

[2] This first talk of this series was presented as a Friday night public lecture in a large auditorium. The rest of the seminar took place in a smaller facility to fewer people.

It's a mistake to think that our mental problems are as vast as the universe, embracing space and sky, and therefore, "Until I destroy the sun and the moon I'll never be able to solve my problems." That's just wrong. We simply need to recognize that we're responsible for solving our own problems because we're responsible for the actions of our body, speech and mind. We can't blame others.

With respect to human problems, most are intellectually generated. Of course, there are problems at the deeper, intuitive level, but most problems, such as emotional disturbances and anxiety, come from the way we think.

When we were babies, we didn't have political problems, did we? When we were babies, we didn't have economic or societal problems. That's because we were too immature for ego conflict or intellectualization. When we were babies we didn't have religious conflict, religious dissatisfaction or philosophical or racial conflict; we didn't have those kinds of intellectual problem.

But as we grow, we begin to intellectualize: "What is society? Who am I? How should I identify myself? What is my significant archetype?" Our ego wants some kind of identity, something to hold on to in a grasping way. It can't be natural. That's why we're completely artificial, confused and dissatisfied.

You can see in the modern world most human problems come from conflicted relationships between people. Men have trouble with women; women have trouble with men. All this comes from intellectual games, not intuition.

Our intellectual concepts fabricate beliefs such as, "This object is the best for me to grasp at. If I can't have it I'll kill myself. Other things are not reality for me; this object is my only reality." In this way we fix our intellectual concepts and finish up committing suicide. So you can see how human intellectual problems are unnatural, unrealistic and completely divorced from reality.

For example, your deluded mind describes an apple as "fantastic. It has a beautiful red color, I love it so much." That's the exaggerated way you describe anything you're attached to and why you finish up with a sick mind. Fundamentally, it's all fantasy; you project your fantasy onto objects and finish up miserable and dissatisfied. You don't relate to the way an object actually exists, only to your fantasized projection of it.

However, from the Buddhist point of view, this gives you the ability to examine your own mind to see if your thinking is positive or negative; to see if your projection is a fantasy or not. You *are* capable of this.

Buddha is one who is totally developed. Each of us has the potential to develop in the same way; we can develop ourselves to the full and eradicate all polluted thought.

When we think about how to cope as a member of society, when we try to be intelligent, figure out how to take advantage of society, of the country and each other, basically, all such thinking comes out of intellectual, artificial, grasping desire. As a result, we end up miserable. This is especially true of modern society, where everybody's trying to cope by intellectualizing and being as intelligent as they can be, but most people still become extreme, miserable and out of control. If you build up this huge fantasy of yourself and how things should be, you reach the point where you cannot cope with that situation. You drown in the ocean of your personal fantasy world. You make it very difficult for yourself.

My suggestion is, therefore, before you reach that state of tremendous confusion, just slowly, slowly try to eliminate the causes and conditions of your confusion. If you do, things will get better and better.

Question whether your intellectual life is good or bad. The Buddhist point of view is that you should question the way you think. Instead of allowing your intellect to rule you, use your discriminating wisdom to analyze whether what you think and do is worthwhile or not.

The reason that I say that our problems—global, societal and personal—are not natural is that they've been built up by our ego's intellectualization. We can see this because when we were babies we didn't have those problems. And when we die, we don't have them either.

The Lens of Meditation

As you know, Tibetan Buddhism places a lot of emphasis on meditation. What meditation does is allow you to see clean clear what's going on in your mind; through it you can see your conventional, superficial ego conflict. That's the purpose of meditation. The moment you meditate you gain access to states of mind beyond your emotional ego conflict. In that way you're able to view your mind as if you were looking at an external object, except here you're seeing what's going on within your mind.

All people have daily problems: ego conflict problems, emotional problems, various obsessions and so forth. We all have problems. But we're also capable of seeing what lies in our mind beyond them. You shouldn't think, "I'm pretty confused. My whole nature must be confusion. I have no hope of releasing my confusion or clearing it up." That's a wrong attitude; it devalues your fundamental human quality.

Buddhist psychology is sort of humanistic. Buddhism is essentially a scientific religion. It focuses on human problems and how to stop them. The emphasis is not on Buddha or God. Therefore, it's worthwhile that we investigate the reality of our own consciousness rather than ignore our mind and place all our attention on our body. That's unhealthy and unbalanced. True satisfaction does not come from the flesh-and-blood body but from the mind. Also, the nature of the mind is completely different from that of the brain.

The reality of our human life is that we are capable of solving our own problems. We should understand very strongly that "My problems are my baby; I have to take care of them myself." By thinking in this way we develop deep self-confidence. How do we come to that understanding? It's because all human beings have wisdom and intelligence. Don't think that human nature is total ignorance. We all have wisdom, love and compassion. Abandon thoughts such as, "I'm a completely angry person; I'm full of hatred. I have no love, no wisdom, no compassion." That's a completely nihilistic view of your reality.

When you trust yourself and feel confident, when you've had some experience of your own wisdom and compassion, you become more natural and allow your intuition to develop, but when you're too intellectual and egotistic you damage your intuition. You're born with intuition intact; your original intuition is uninfluenced by philosophy, religion, teachers or the environment. It's there but it has to be protected in such a way that it's allowed to function without being shut down and suppressed.

As I said above, we should recognize that we humans create all our own problems. We cannot blame society, parents or friends. We create all our own problems and suffering; therefore, we can create our own liberation.

If we die a natural death, during the process, all our concepts—political, economic, societal, racial, capitalist, communist and so forth—naturally go into space and disappear. Anything we think about, any selfish attitude with which we take advantage of other people by thinking that we're intelligent and they're foolish, dissolves into space. And not only at the time of death—the process of going to sleep is similar to that of a natural death with respect to the absorption of the elements and concepts. In other words, every time we go to sleep, even then all our ego conflicts as well as the various concepts I mentioned before dissolve. That's why it's better just to go to sleep rather than get all emotional, stressed, agitated and angry. In sleep we go into a natural, fundamental state of consciousness in which our intellect no longer functions.

Therefore, in the Buddhist tradition, we prefer to meditate early in the morning because during the night all our polluted concepts have disappeared and our mind is a little clearer then than later in the day. During the day the energy of polluted concepts builds up;

during sleep they subside. When we awaken they return slowly, but they're usually hidden from our view. So, when we meditate early, our mind is more neutral than extreme and our concentration tends to be better than at later times, when it's more sluggish and distracted.

Actually this doesn't apply only to meditation. Even if you're not a meditator, when you have something you want to think about clearly, you're better off doing it early in the morning. Also, Buddhist meditation doesn't mean only single-pointed concentration; we have analytical meditation on reality as well.

However, no matter who you are, it's very important to know how your mind works in daily life, while you're asleep and during the death process. It's essential that you educate yourself in this. If you do, you'll have no fear that dying is horrible, like falling into a black hole; that death's a black hole that's going to suck you in and eat you up.

From the moment we were born we've been destined for death. We think that dying is a big deal, worse than losing a job, a boyfriend, a girlfriend, husband or wife. That's the wrong attitude. We think that dying is negative, but that's just our projection.

Death is better than a flower, for example. A flower cannot give you tremendous peace and bliss. It can give you something, but not that. Death, however, can give you both: tremendous peace and tremendous bliss. Death is better than your boyfriend, girlfriend, husband or wife because they give you very little bliss. They cannot truly solve your problems. They can alleviate emotional anxiety momentarily, perhaps, but not for long. At the moment of death, however, all anxiety and other emotional problems are totally cut off for a long period of time.

The process of a natural death is actually quite slow. Each of the four elements—earth, water, fire and air—deteriorates, or absorbs; the five aggregates—form, feeling, discrimination, compositional factors and consciousness—also absorb; and the dying person gradually goes through the experience of a series of internal hallucinatory visions.

Normally we think that looking at visual objects is a fantastic pleasure, a necessary sensation. We think it's important and grasp at such objects as much as we can. The Buddhist idea is that we be as detached as possible from sense objects.

Loosening up

I'm sure you've heard of renunciation. Actually, it's a most natural thing. Why? When you were a baby you didn't have the kinds of problems that you do now; you didn't have the societal attachment that you've now built up within yourself; you didn't have all the sensory objects that you do now. When you were in your mother's womb you'd already renounced everything; you had no external objects to grasp at. You didn't have even one grape! You were naturally renounced.

Not being renounced means, for example, you have one car—that's not enough. You have two cars—that's not enough either; you need a boat. You have a boat but that's not enough—you need a bigger one. Your wants are infinite; that's the nature of dissatisfaction. But when you're born you're born with renunciation. What I mean is that at that time you don't have much grasping, you don't have so much to worry about. You arrive in the world relatively free. But then you build up your attachments and with them your worries. Then you die and again naturally renounce. So, be natural. Don't think that the renunciation and detachment Eastern philosophy talks about are some kind of polluted Oriental ideas.

Satisfaction does not depend on material objects; satisfaction comes from simplicity. I'm not saying this because I'm jealous of people from rich economies; I'm not saying wealthy people are bad. Nevertheless, rich or poor, we all need simplicity to experience inner satisfaction. I'm not jealous of Westerners' pleasures or wealth.

The question is, why are you dissatisfied? You always lay the blame outside—"This is not enough; that's not sufficient." That's not true. Something's missing inside of you. That's what you have to recognize.

When I refer to detachment I don't mean you need to totally renounce. Being detached means being a little more easy-going, not hanging on too tightly. It means making yourself a little bit loose instead of always being uptight. Loosen up.

Therefore, when I say that Swiss people should renounce I don't mean that you have to give away all your money. You can lead a happy life with money as long as you enjoy it in a reasonable way with some kind of appreciation for life by looking at the lives of people in the Third World. If you just hoard your Swiss francs, you'll become very unhappy with your objects of pleasure. Instead, you should appreciate your Swiss money and pleasures in a relaxed kind of way: "I should enjoy what I have and be satisfied." Think like that. Otherwise, even if you have all the money in Switzerland you won't be happy; all it will do is make you miserable.

According to Buddhist psychology, whether or not an object satisfies you depends on the decision made by your mind. If you've already decided, "This is nice; it makes me happy," then whenever your eye contacts whatever it is, you think, "Oh, that's nice." If your mind has already decided, "He's a very bad guy," whenever you see him you automatically think, "Oh, he's bad."

Why does Tibetan Buddhism teach us to understand the death process and train us to deal with it? It's so that when the time of crisis arrives and the various illusory visions arise, instead of being confused, we'll know what's going on and will recognize illusions as illusions, projections as projections and fantasies as fantasies.

After the four elements have dissolved and disappeared and the breathing has stopped, the subtle consciousness still remains. At this point Western doctors will say that the patient is dead and put him in the freezer but from the Buddhist point of view, even though the person's not breathing, he's still alive, with four visions yet to come: the white, red, black and clear light. These visions arise after the breathing has completely stopped. Accomplished meditators recognize these visions as they come and go and can remain for many days or even months in the blissful clear light state, in direct contact with universal reality, free of any polluted view.

Skeptical Westerners will say, "This is just the Buddhist faith; this monk's just talking about what he believes; it has nothing to do with us," but that's not true. This is human experience, although it may not be yours.

Did you hear about the French man who was pronounced dead by his doctors but two hours later woke up and subsequently wrote about his experience of death? He wasn't a religious man, a believer, he knew nothing about Buddhism, but still, he was thought to be dead for two hours and after that time awoke.

However, whether or not you believe what Buddhism says about the death process, an easy way to understand it is to become familiar with the process of going to sleep. That's a good example of what happens at the time of death. I believe that now there's even scientific equipment that can monitor the sleep process and the dissolution of concepts at that time, so by conducting this kind of analysis you can become familiar with the process without having to rely on the Buddhist explanation. If you understand this you can easily relate it to the death process.

We've run out of time and I don't want to keep you too long, but in case what I've said has made you more confused I'd better take some questions.

Q. Humans only know things by comparison. For example, we only know hot because of cold and *vice versa*. Similarly, it seems necessary to have bad things in order to appreciate the good. In that case it is likely that imperfection is part of the perfection of the creation to which it permits movement. How do you consider it possible to eliminate the bad and keep only the good?

Lama. You don't need to worry that there'll be no good if there's no bad. Miserable thinking is what's bad. Of course, I agree that miserable and happy are interdependent conditions, but you can see that you can eliminate a certain degree of misery and generate more happiness. You can experience that for yourself.

Q. Can you talk about possible conflicts that might arise for a Christian who wants to use Buddhist methods?

Lama. That's no problem. Again, Buddhism and Christianity come from the intellect. Why? There may be some slight philosophical differences between them but philosophy is a bit like clothing. Swiss people wear suits; Tibetans wear *chubas*. On the other hand, some Swiss like yak butter and I like Swiss cheese and chocolate. So what?

I have many elderly lady students in Indiana, America, who are Christian, but we teach them Buddhism, how to meditate, the meaning of life. We are dealing with life every day and Buddhism can help with that. Buddhism is not against God; Buddhism is not against Buddha. Buddhism simply talks about the daily problems humans face. These old ladies—some of them are around eighty years old—told me that Buddhism enhances their understanding of the Bible: "I didn't really understand the Bible before, but Buddhism has helped me do so." They've really told me that. This is my anthropological research!

Let's take problems for example. Buddhism says the mind is the creator of problems; Christianity says that God created everything. For me, there's no contradiction. The Christian doctrine of God as the creator of everything is good for the Western mind because otherwise the Western ego thinks, "I made everything." Western individualism is so powerful. Westerners think they are the creator or the principal force, so that when they hear, "God is the creator, not you," they slow down. The Buddhist explanation is also good: when we hear that the creator of our problems is our own mind, we don't blame Lord Buddha.

So I definitely agree. Of course, I'm not well educated in the Christian Bible, but still, I have studied it to a certain extent and I've studied a little Buddhism, so from my point of view the essence of Christianity and the essence of Buddhism go together without contradiction.

For example, let's say European Buddhist people think, "Buddhism has meditation; I like that. Christianity has no meditation." That's a wrong conception. European Buddhists think, "I've found Buddhism; Buddhism is very good. I can meditate every day; I can even meditate in the bathroom. I don't need to go to church. Christianity has no meditation." Their egos are proud to have found Buddhism. That's just wrong because they don't understand that in fact Christianity does have meditation. Unfortunately they're simply ignorant of their own country's religion.

Q. Why is a baby crying when he's hungry if he's completely detached?
Lama. Oh, good debate. A baby cries because it's hungry. But a baby doesn't cry because he lost his wife or girlfriend. And a baby doesn't cry for chocolate like we do. Do you think babies have political problems? Not enough wages? Can't find a job? OK, I think that's clear.

Q. Many people have had experiences similar to death while on drugs. What do you think?

Lama. I think that's a good example. That's human experience. I think it helps them understand that the human being is not only the body, that besides the body there's the consciousness, which is actually the nuclear essence of the human being. But drugs can also make you lose your memory, for example. So taking drugs has an up side and a down. However, once you've had a drug experience you're better off not doing it again. It's like once you've had a bad experience with a girlfriend you should avoid that in future too.

Q. I thought that the consciousness of the dream state was gross but you said that the intellect disappears when we dream. I would like to understand this better.

Lama. First you go to sleep, then, when all four elements have dissolved and so forth you reach the clear light. At that point you manifest a dream body, which is like being in a nightclub! But sleep and dream are different. From sleep you have to manifest a dream body, then the dream mind can function. When you awaken, the process goes in reverse: the elements of the dream body absorb, you return to sleep and then gradually wake up. What I want you to understand is that the states of sleep and dream are different.

Q. Does the dream state produce karma? Do we create karma as we dream?

Lama. Yes, we do. In tantra we say that death is like going to sleep, and passing from death into the intermediate state [Tib:

bardo] is like dreaming because there's a certain similarity in the experiences.

When we die, the elements of the gross body absorb. Similarly, when we go to sleep, our gross body and concepts absorb. Then, when we're asleep we enter a kind of clear light experience and then manifest a subtle body, the dream state body, which is similar in nature to the bardo body and acts in a way similar to the bardo.

The dream state body is more subtle than our normal body; the dream state mind is more subtle than the waking state mind. Buddhist meditators have much experience of the dream state mind being far more clean clear than the waking state mind when it comes to seeing into the future and things like that. Also, we say that whatever expresses itself in your dreams, whatever pictures you get, totally relate to what's going on in your waking state life, and we don't say that what you experience in your waking state has greater reality than what happens in your dreams. Both experiences are equally real.

Q. Since all of us have the capacity to go beyond problems, can we say that beings can be unhappy only when they can think, use their intellect, cry or just say whatever they like?

Lama. Well, your question isn't all that clear to me but in a way, I agree. If people do not have discriminating wisdom as to what they should think and what they should not, then whatever garbage thoughts come into their mind just gush out verbally and manifest physically as well. Everything comes out and this can create very heavy karma. But humans have the ability to change their thought patterns. If the thought of insulting somebody arises we have to control it; we should not just say whatever comes into our head. That's wrong.

Westerners have the misconception that they should do whatever their mind tells them; say whatever they want. This is totally extreme. Your mind is like a mad elephant; what kind of damage will that do if you let it run wild? Since you realize that you have an egotistic mad elephant mind, be careful. Doing what it wants, saying whatever you think, doesn't mean that you're open. That's mistaken openness from my point of view—if you open your accumulated garbage, it stinks! If you release your nuclear missile, watch out!

Our thoughts have a long history. They don't come out of nowhere, just like that. Thoughts are like clouds. Clouds require many conditions to come together: moisture, wind and so forth. Thoughts are like that; they need cooperative conditions, interdependent ideas and then they come. So when you see certain undesirable thoughts starting to form, you can cut them off before they develop.

Thank you very much. I hope I have not created more confusion for you. We're all working together for peace and liberation, so I'm very happy about that.

··· 3 ···

The Nature of the Mind

ACH HUMAN BEING has a mind, and that mind has three divisions: gross, subtle and most subtle. Similarly, we have a body, and that too has three divisions: gross, subtle and most subtle.

The gross consciousness comprises the five sensory consciousnesses that we use every day. The subtle consciousness can include things like intuitive ego and intuitive superstition. They're subtle in the sense that we can't see or understand them clearly. The gross mind is so busy that it obscures the subtle. When the gross mind is no longer flashing, or functioning, the subtle mind then has a chance to arise. And that's one of the functions of Tibetan Buddhist tantra: it eliminates the gross concepts, giving the subtle mind space to function. That's the business of tantra.

Also, the gross mind has no strength, no power. Even though it understands certain things, it's relatively weak. The subtle mind has much more power to penetrate and comprehend.

Meditation cuts the gross, busy mind and allows the subtle consciousness to function. In that way it performs a similar function to that of death. However, to do the kind of meditation that leads us through the death process, we need strong single-pointed concentration.

As you know, Buddhism explains emptiness [Skt: *shunyata*], the nature of universal reality. We experience emptiness when we have eliminated the gross, superficial, conventional mind, allowing it to manifest. Even people who have never heard of emptiness and have no idea what it is experience great emptiness in their mind during the death process when all their busy minds have dissolved. The moment your gross, crowded concepts stop, you feel some space, emptiness. There's nothing you actually empty, but because your concepts are so crowded, because your mind is so full, when all that content disappears you experience emptiness.

Sometimes when Buddhist philosophers describe shunyata— "Blah, blah, blah, blah, blah"—it sounds so complicated. And it's true; Buddhist philosophy can be very sophisticated. Ordinary people don't understand. "How can I possibly understand shunyata? Nagarjuna says, 'Blah, blah, blah'; Chandrakirti says, 'Blah, blah, blah.'" But when we really bring it back down to earth, all we're saying is, when you cut your crowded superstitions, the experience will come; when you eliminate all your busy concepts, the experience of shunyata will arise, as it does in the death process.

At the moment we're normally far from reality—from the reality of ourselves, the reality of all that exists—because we're enveloped by a heavy blanket of superstition. One blanket of superstition; two blankets of superstition; three blankets of superstition...this blanket, that blanket, another blanket.... All these gross blankets, gross minds, completely built up, like Mt. Meru, like Mt. Everest—so heavy that you can't shake them off.

Now, I don't know what methods you normally use, but our

business this weekend is to look at the Buddhist method of slowly, slowly removing these blankets one by one: meditation. And in order to do that, we have to understand the characteristic nature of our own mind.

First of all, the mind is not a material substance; it has no shape or color. It's a kind of formless, colorless energy: the energy of thought or consciousness. Therefore its nature is clean clear and it takes the reflection of phenomena inside. Even thoughts you consider to be heavy and negative still have their own essence, their own clarity, in order to perceive reality or reflect projections.

Also, consciousness, or mind, is like space. The essence of space is its own nature, unmixed with pollution or clouds. The nature of clouds, or pollution, and the nature of space are different—even though pollution pervades space.

The reason why I'm mentioning the negative mind is that humans have a tendency to harbor preconceptions such as "I'm a bad person, my mind is bad, I'm too negative." We always criticize ourselves in a dualistic way. Buddhism says that that's wrong. The characteristic nature of space is not pollution; the nature of pollution is not space. Similarly, the nature of the consciousness is not negative. In fact, the Buddha himself said that buddha nature lies within each of us and its nature is pure, clean and clear. Also, Maitreya explained that if you put a diamond in *kaka*, its nature remains different from that of kaka and the nature of the kaka remains different from that of the diamond.

It's important to know this. A clean clear mind exists within us; the fundamental nature of our consciousness is pure. But while our mind has its own essence of clarity, it's covered by a contaminating heavy blanket of concepts. Nevertheless, its nature is still clean clear; our consciousness is clean clear. Therefore we have to recognize, "My nature, the essence of my consciousness, is not totally negative. The pure, clean clear nature of my mind exists within me right now."

Actually, our consciousness has two characteristics, relative and absolute, and the nature of the relative is not negativity or superstition.

Christians might say that the human soul is pure, not negative. It is free of ego conflict, craving-desire, hatred and jealousy. Similarly, the relative human consciousness can go from whatever level it's currently at all the way up to enlightenment. That doesn't mean that ego conflict goes all the way to enlightenment; the dissatisfied, emotionally restless mind never goes through the first, second, third and other bodhisattva levels to the tenth and then enlightenment. That doesn't happen.

The essence of the human consciousness or, we can say, the essence of the human soul, continuously goes up, up and up. The negative blanket of superstition never goes up. Each time we purify our negativities they just disappear, disappear, disappear....

So, that's the relative. With respect to the absolute nature of human consciousness, or soul, it is totally nondual. In the nonduality of the human mind there's no mixed up confusion or emotional disturbance. No such thing exists; its nature is always clean clear. Therefore we should understand that the nuclear essence of each of us is our consciousness and that consciousness is not mixed with negativity. It has its own nature, both relative and absolute.

Sometimes we liken the mind to the ocean, where ego conflicts are like waves upon the surface. Concepts arise like waves, shake things up a bit and then subside back into the ocean of consciousness. So the consciousness of each of us is clean clear in nature and our craving desire, hatred and ignorance are like waves upon the surface. That means we have the capacity not to shake our consciousness; to some extent we can hold it without shaking. That's what meditation does.

Now, with respect to motivation, negative motivation is also like a wave. It creates all the confusion, dissatisfaction, pain and misery we experience. All that comes from the negative motivation in our mind—that's the root of all human problems. It's most worthwhile to investigate this directly for yourself.

Still, we should understand that our own nature is not totally negative, not totally hopeless. We should respect our own nature, our own purity, our own characteristics. When we respect ourselves we respect others. If we interpret ourselves as a big hassle, selfish, totally hopeless and negative, we interpret others in the same way. That's dangerous.

Meditation

When you meditate, it's not your sense perception or sense consciousness that's meditating. Western people sometimes get confused about this because they're so used to the sense world being their only reality; out of habit, Western mentality is that reality is limited to what you can see, touch and so forth. But the sense consciousness is foolish. It does not have the intelligence to discriminate between right and wrong. That's why as soon as we open our eyes we're distracted by sense objects and the flashing of dualistic concepts. To avoid these foolish old habits of the senses I always recommend that you meditate with your eyes naturally closed.

You can see why. Your mind always wants to see beautiful things. It has already decided. Say you're planning to go to the market. Before you leave home you start visualizing: "Apples are beautiful this time of year. Pears would be good too." So when you get to the market and see the apples and pears, they appear beautiful because of your preconceptions.

Sense perception is like the Swiss population; consciousness is like the Swiss government. The Swiss government decides, "These people are good; those are bad." The decision is made. The consciousness is like that. Our preconceptions decide ahead of time what objects are good or bad, so when the sense consciousness contacts those objects it sees them as good or bad. That's why I say that sense perception is foolish—it doesn't have its own strength and discrimination.

Moreover, sense perception sees only the gross reality. It has no way of understanding totality. Modern science tries to understand things by looking at them with ever more powerful microscopes but you can never penetrate their essence that way. Buddhism knows well that you can never understand emptiness like that.

So this afternoon we are going to meditate on our own consciousness. But don't be afraid: "How can I meditate? I don't know what my consciousness is. This monk's telling me to meditate on my consciousness, but my problem is that I don't know what it is. How can I meditate on it?"

Well, say, for example, you're in a room where you can't see the sun directly but you can see its rays coming in through the window. From seeing the rays, you can understand that the sun exists. Similarly, from experiencing your thoughts and motivations you can understand that your consciousness underlies them.

Looking at or simply being aware of your thoughts and motivations is good enough for you to be meditating on your own consciousness. Is that clear? I'll say it again. One way of meditating on your consciousness is simply to be aware of your mind's view. When you look at your own mind's view, when you are aware of your own mind's view, that's good enough. I call that meditation on your consciousness.

Another way of doing this is to be aware of the essence of your own thoughts. You know the moment you close your eyes some kind of thought is going to arise—just be aware of its essence. I also call that meditation on your consciousness. Don't worry whether your thoughts are good or bad—the essential aspect of both is clear, because both good thoughts and bad reflect phenomena.

When I say "meditation" I don't mean that you should squeeze yourself. These days there are a lot of misconceptions about what meditation is, especially in the West. Some people think it means you should squeeze yourself tightly or even shake; others think it means you should just completely go loose. Both are wrong. With one, you're completely distracted; with the other you're completely sluggish.

Meditation is actually very simple. When you close your eyes, what happens is that your awareness begins to radiate, like a sensitive radar detector. A good radar detector picks up any kind of signal; it notices, it's aware. Similarly, when you meditate your mind becomes aware; you become very sensitive or totally awake as to what's going on. That's what I call meditation—intensive conscious awareness. But I don't mean that in the conversational sense: "Blah, blah, blah, oh, there's a light, there's something else." It's not like that.

However, I'd better explain what I mean by conversation. Let's say we're supposed to be meditating. We're aware of what's going on around us: a car goes by; there goes a truck.... We're aware, but then what we should not do is start some kind of conversation about what we've noticed: "That must be a very nice truck. Perhaps it's full of cheese or juice for sale." Conversation. That's what we should not do. We should be aware but in control and not start some kind of internal dialog.

In meditation you're learning how to control and eventually eliminate the uncontrolled mind. Why are you out of control? It's because your mind generates conversations: "He's like this; she's like that. He says this; I don't like it. She says that; I like it." All this kind of internal chatter is what I mean by conversation. The uncontrolled mind is constantly reacting but the controlled mind does not react at all. Somebody calls you a bad person but you don't react, you don't make conversation: "She said I'm bad. That hurt my ego, hurt my ego, hurt my ego, hurt my ego...." That's what I mean by reacting; that's an uncontrolled mind, a mind obsessed.

The way I look at it, an obsessed mind has two objects: the beautiful object of craving desire or the repulsive object of aversion. And a mind obsessed with such objects cannot move away from them. That means you're not free, not flexible. You're always thinking,

"This, this, this, this, this…." That's what obsessed means. And whether it's an object of hatred or jealousy or craving desire, an obsessed mind is disturbed. Meditation teaches us to break the habit of reacting when an object of obsession appears.

Now, you may ask, what really is the benefit of awareness of your own consciousness as opposed to, say, awareness of a flower or a girlfriend or a boyfriend? There's benefit in using the nature of your consciousness to generate awareness because, unlike boyfriends, girlfriends and flowers, consciousness doesn't stimulate notions of concrete self-existence. Therefore, the beauty of watching, or being aware of, your own consciousness is that it leads to the breakdown of your heavy blanket, superstitious concepts and to the experience of great emptiness.

In order to solve our problems we need some experience. Intellectual "blah, blah" understanding is not enough. To break down concepts we need a way of gaining experience with our own mind, and when we've had such an experience we know that we're really capable of solving our own problems. This encourages us: "I can do anything I want. I can really solve my problems." From the Buddhist point of view, that's the start of human liberation.

Normally we're too intellectual. We're constantly saying, "Good, bad, good, bad, good, bad." When we meditate, we stop saying, "Good, bad, good, bad, good, bad." The intellectual good-bad thinking gets stopped. Good-bad thinking is dualistic; it splits your mind. Just be aware; just be conscious.

We should be like the sun or the moon. They don't think, "I'll make people warm; I'll give people light. How grateful they'll be."

That's not what they do and that's how we should be: intensively aware without any intellectual good or bad. That's very important.

Maitreya Buddha said that written texts and scriptures are like a bridge. In order to cross a river you need a reliable bridge. Once you've crossed the river you can say, "Bye-bye bridge." If instead you start thinking, "Oh, this bridge is so kind, this bridge is so kind, this bible is so kind, this sutra is so kind," if you get so attached to the scripture, it doesn't make sense.

So what I'm saying is that from a certain point of view, intellectual good-bad is OK—it's good to be able to discriminate between good and bad; that has some value—but always going "good, bad, good, bad, good, bad" doesn't have much worth. You need some discriminating wisdom but at a certain point you have to go beyond it, leave it and just be.

Let go; just be

I said before that the experience of awareness of your own consciousness leads to the experience of nonduality. That might make you want to argue, "How can that lead to nonduality? There are two flowers there all the time; the sun and moon are both there all the time. There are crowds of people everywhere. How can I experience nonduality? Duality is always there."

That's true. However, although we experience duality is at the conventional level of reality, that doesn't mean when we experience nonduality we become nihilists. It means we have a broad understanding of reality and the conventional world no longer sends vibrations through our mind.

That's why you should not debate with yourself when you try to experience nonduality: "How can there be no duality? I can see two flowers." At that time you have to put a stop to such debating minds. When meditating on nonduality you have to stop that kind of conversation. We're trying to experience something, not destroy the flower. We're trying to develop some kind of awareness and understand the totality of the flower. When you attain single-pointed concentration on the nonduality of the flower, at that moment of experience the flower disappears. The conventional flower disappears in the experience.

Similarly, when you're experiencing the nonduality of yourself, there's no concept of the hopeless you in that moment. That disappears. There's no plaintive "Am I beautiful or ugly?" That kind of relative conversation disappears. At that moment there's no thought of cosmetics; there's no worry about not being beautiful enough. There are, however, fewer wrinkles—the less you worry the fewer your wrinkles!

Anyway, here I'm talking about the stage of conscious experience. But don't worry, thinking, "I'm disappearing, everything's disappearing; maybe I'm going to end up a nihilist." Don't worry about that. Just completely knock out all your wrong conceptions; destroy the entire kingdom of egotistic conceptions.

In this kind of meditation—intensive awareness of your own consciousness without interpretation, whether it's good consciousness or bad—just be. And let go. Again, letting go doesn't mean a spaced out letting go; it means intensive awareness. Intensive awareness is like the sun—the radiant consciousness is there; then just let go, just be, let go. That's good enough.

Also, when you close your eyes, just relax your awareness. Sometimes different colors come; different visions come. Don't make conversation with white color or anything else; just be.

In other words, whatever your experience of your consciousness, whatever that moment of experience, just remember that; just remember that one moment; stay with that memory. The continuity of the memory of awareness of your consciousness is good enough.

To conclude, what I'm trying to explain is that this weekend we're simply trying to experience something. If you have a meditative experience of knocking out your blanket of superstition, this weekend course will have been worthwhile; if you don't, it will not have been. That's how I feel and it's my human right to tell you.

Now, you don't have to believe anything I say. There's neither requirement nor obligation for you to do so. Simply try to experience. "This monk says that there's an experience to be had. Is there or not?" That's all you have to find out. But without meditation experience, you cannot be liberated. In that case, Buddhism cannot help.

Do you understand? It's very simple. You don't have to become a great meditator. Just relax and be conscious. Don't use your sense perception's good and bad; just be aware of your own consciousness without any interpretation. Just be. Even if bad thoughts come, don't worry about them. And don't reject them. The essence of bad thoughts is still the clean clear consciousness.

And don't engage any objects that arise in conversation. Doing so is the worst enemy of meditation. [Lama picks up a huge mango from his side-table.] You're supposed to be aware of your own consciousness but suddenly the thought of something else arises [Lama holds up the mango]. When it does, don't reject it: "Oh, that's a horrible thought." Don't get upset at the appearance of that thought. Just observe its essence within; just be aware at the subjective level. Don't engage in any kind of conversation [examining mango closely]: "What's this? Is it mine? Oh, it's yellow; it's so beautiful. Look at this; fantastic." Don't converse about the object.

It's very important for meditators not to generate discursive thoughts of "this, this, this," making some kind of normal conversation. Stop that. Just be conscious of the thought; just be aware of it. If you are, that thought can lead you beyond distraction to nonduality. Are you completely clean clear about this?

So, to conclude, when you meditate, first check your motivation. If you feel it's a bit crazy, spend a little time doing breathing meditation. Breathe naturally and focus on your breath. After a while turn your attention to your own thought. That's good enough. Thank you very much.

··· 4 ···

The Death Process

DURING OUR LIFETIME we accumulate a great many hallucinated experiences that cause us to experience much confusion at the time of death. Since these are interdependent phenomena, when we are old and our four elements absorb, these experiences energize internal chaos.

Actually, as we age, our sense organ function declines, so in a sense our four elements have already begun to absorb. Our eyes and ears start to fail and our other sense organs can also produce confusion.

If you've received teachings on the death process before you've probably heard terms like the earth element "sinks," or "absorbs," or "dissolves." It means that the earth element deteriorates. That's why old people have impaired senses and can't see or hear properly. Their earth element has begun to deteriorate. Of course, we see this not only in old people; it happens to the young as well.

Not only do our sense organs deteriorate; so do our sense enjoyments. Sense objects no longer bring pleasure. For example, if we are suffering from a serious disease, things that used to give us pleasure, like food, visual objects and so forth, no longer do so. Flowers that we used to enjoy no longer please and might even annoy us: "I hate those red flowers. Get them out of here."

When our four elements deteriorate we experience certain internal visions. First there's the hallucination of a mirage; then there's a vision of smoke; then sparks of fire. These are all internal experiences; there's no actual water or fire in the room. Still, dying people can say, "Take that water away" or "Stop that fire." All this produces internal confusion—in our mind, we experience fire; we feel as if it's coming toward us and that we're going to get burnt. Although these are hallucinations, we feel as if the water or fire are really there and get very confused.

Our ego normally grasps at certain external objects, but here, the moment we experience them they disappear. This brings more confusion and hallucination and we get very scared. And at the same time we're especially afraid of losing our ego identity.

Let me explain this again. When we're in the experience of our four elements sinking, our five sense organs are deteriorating and, for us, our external sense objects are also deteriorating. But we want to hang onto them, just as in life we grasp strongly at objects of attachment. At death time all these things start to disappear, we begin to lose our identity and become terrified.

Usually our companions and possessions are part of our identity and having them close by makes us feel secure. When we're dying, everything internal and external deteriorates and disappears, so we get very scared because we're losing our normal security.

However, through educating ourselves in the death process and training our mind in meditation, when the death experience comes we're able to recognize what's going on and think, "It's the conditions that are making me hallucinate. There are no self-existent hallucinated objects." Thus this also enhances our understanding of emptiness.

Losing the ego

So, what is the self-existent I? The self-existent I does not exist; don't think that it does. In this way, we first try to educate you with words: "There is no dualistic I." We push you intellectually, "There's no self-existent I." But at the time of death, this understanding is not pushed intellectually; you lose your self-existent identity naturally.

Some people experience loss of identity in meditation and get scared. That's good. You should be scared. Tibetan monks want to scare you. Westerners don't like to be scared but we have the skills to make you afraid! Many people have this experience. That's good.

Why are you afraid? Why are you afraid of losing something? What you're losing is your self-existent or concrete preconception of yourself; that's what's shaken. It's your projection of yourself that shakes, not your nonduality. Your own true nature isn't shaken.

Once, Lama Je Tsongkhapa was giving a discourse on emptiness. While he was talking, one of his close disciples suddenly experienced emptiness right at that moment and grabbed at his lapel because he felt himself disappearing. Feeling completely lost and totally shaken, he grabbed his shirt to make sure he was still there. That's how it should be: experiences and realizations should come during teachings. The way to discover your own true nature is to break the fantasy, or preconceived ideas, of yourself. But don't misunderstand what I'm saying; the English language has different ways of interpreting the words "self" and "losing the self."

When I use the word "preconceived" I mean you're fixing your reality: "I am this, I am that, I am the other, this is me," creating a strong preconceived idea of who you are, what you are. That's what I mean by "self." That self is non-existent. It's merely a projection of your own ego.

For example, a man identifies himself as such and such a woman's husband. In this way he gives himself the flavor of a self-existent husband. As soon as he decides that he's this concrete, self-existent husband, he immediately projects onto his wife that she too is a concrete, self-existent wife. These concrete preconceptions lead to misery. "My existence depends on my wife. If she disappears, so do I." He identifies himself as a concrete husband and her as a concrete wife, and then his life becomes impossible. Because the truth of the situation is that both he and his wife are impermanent, transitory, changing from day to day. In other words, he overestimates reality.

These days we see a lot of confusion among young people. "Society wants me to be someone: an engineer, a scientist." They feel they need a profession with which they can identify. Part of them believes it; another part does not. So they're confused. Nevertheless, they do want some kind of identity so they create their own. They drop out, take drugs and become hippies. That doesn't mean they're free of ego. They already have an ego but they want another layer to it with which they can identify. They already have a self-existent I; they want to add an extra flavor to that.

It's quite easy to experience the self-existent imagination of yourself I'm talking about. It's not difficult. Right now you can observe and analyze your self-imagined identity. And because you have preconceptions about this self you get into trouble. You always criticize yourself: "I'm not good enough." If you analyze this way of thinking you will understand how you're deluded and out of touch with reality. You can understand right now.

Because you cling to such a limited projection of yourself, such a limited self-image, this becomes the root of all your other limitations. You have limited love, limited wisdom and limited compassion. Because you've already decided that fundamentally, you're narrow, your whole life becomes narrow—your wisdom becomes narrow, your love becomes narrow, everything about you becomes narrow. Just because of your fundamentally narrow projection of yourself.

At the time of death, when your four elements absorb, all your gross concepts about yourself, your pleasures, environment, friends, self-pity love and compassion disappear. That's why we say that when your air element absorbs into your consciousness, your eighty superstitions disappear.[3]

When your eighty superstitions, your eighty ego-aspects, stop, internally, your conscious experience is that of vast emptiness, a great empty space. It's like the clear blue sky, totally empty space, clean clear space: this is what you experience internally. Why? Because normally our mind is crowded with concepts, the eighty deluded superstitions; so crowded that there's no space to see

---

[3] See *Death, Intermediate State and Rebirth*, p. 38 ff.

reality. At that moment in the death process, all these dualistic concepts disappear. The result is that you touch a broader reality.

Inner experiences at the time of death

Normally our physical energy also runs in the wrong direction, causing our delusions and superstitions to explode, but at the time of death this energy naturally integrates into our *shushuma*, or central channel, and brings an experience of great peace and emptiness. Therefore, tantra emphasizes the importance of meditating on the *nadis* (psychic channels) and *chakras* (wheels, or energy centers) and drawing the energy into the central channel.

If you focus strongly with penetrative concentration on one of your chakras—heart, navel, throat, crown or brow—energy is drawn to that spot instead of going in the wrong direction. So yogis and yoginis control their energy by meditating on the chakras in their central channel and thus simulate the death experience in meditation.

Following the absorption of the four elements, our breathing stops completely, but after that, four visions still arise: the white, red, black and clear light visions.

Now, from the moment of conception we have had within us fundamental male and female energies received from our father and mother respectively. That's why tantra says that each of us always has within us the union of these fundamental male and female energies.

The white vision happens because our male energy is drawn into our central channel and as a reflection of this white energy, our consciousness experiences a great empty space full of radiant white light. Similarly, the red vision happens through the drawing of our female energy into our central channel, resulting in our consciousness experiencing a vast emptiness pervaded by red light.

After the red vision ceases, because now all light has stopped, the black vision arises for a short time. When that stops, the clear light vision arises. Again, it is only an experience; at that time there's no Swiss chocolate. We experience a gigantic empty space that is pervaded by an impression of clear light. Since it's just an experience, we call it the clear light experience. At that moment there are no sensory objects whatsoever in view—no sensory colors, no beautiful sense objects; no material sense objects at all. No Geneva ladies; no Geneva gentlemen; no Geneva shops; no UN meetings—completely numb; no busy Geneva at all.

All our objects of pride have gone, as have all objects of desire, hatred and jealousy; all objects of ego have completely disappeared. All depressed vision has gone, all black vision has gone—the only vision left is that of light, the clear light vision.

Now, this is important. Most of the time, we're not aware, and because we're so deluded, inflexible, confused and impure, our sense consciousness always experiences a kind of darkness. If we were clean clear, we'd always have a light in front of us. Actually, I truly believe that that experience is always with us but we ignore it— we're so deluded that we don't see it. When our mind is clean clear, some kind of light projection arises; as long as we remain confused and impure, polluted projections will always come into our mind or manifest in front of us. This is important to know—right now!

Now, I would really like to know, how many people here have had that kind of experience? Let do; let do like this [asking everybody to raise their hands]: how many of you have had that kind of experience? I've said this many times before. When you're depressed and impure and your mind has degenerated, even outdoors you have some kind of polluted projection. The sun may be shining but you still have a polluted projection. However, when you're clean clear and pure within and look at something, outside of you there's a vision of light. That's what I'm talking about. So how many of you have had that kind of experience?

This is very simple. I'm not talking about higher realizations. Just be conscious of how confused you are in your daily life and how your confusion brings no external reflection, or of how clean clear you are within and how that does bring an external reflection. Analyze your experiences of this. It's a very simple thing; it's not some kind of great meditational experience. It's a question of sensitivity.

When you are so degenerate, too negative, you can see in your daily life that something happens to your view of the world outside of you. Conversely, when you're clean clear and pure, your external view is something else. This is important. It's not something higher; it's a question of sensitivity. We always talk about negative and positive, don't we? That's our business; it concerns all of us. We have to try to be as positive as possible and then analyze the resultant vibration.

This is logical. Let me explain it another way. Many high lamas' biographies explain that they always had pure visions of deities. They always had pure vision of Lord Buddha, Manjushri or other deities arising in front of them, but what always comes to us? Objects of anger, craving desire, ignorance, jealousy and so forth. That's simple and logical. We're all human beings but some always get pure visions, others get negative visions. This is logical; it's not complicated.

If every month you're conscious or aware of the patterns of your mind's visions, the rhythm and view of your consciousness, you can analyze what's going on with you. It's not difficult. Since we are seeking inner experiences we have to know what's going on in our mind. So it's very useful to analyze our visions and dreams in this way. That's how we come to understand karma. We often listen to teachings on karma—"Karma is this, blah, blah, blah; karma is that, blah, blah, blah"—but we're not convinced. But when we experience our own karma with our own understanding and awareness, when we see what's going on in our mind and life, month by month and year by year, that makes us really understand karma.

You may have heard about many of the great meditators who are able to remain in meditation for long periods at the time of death. When the death process brings them to the clear light, they concentrate on that and can stay in it for days, weeks or even months. That's possible; that's the point. Even after their breathing has stopped, they can remain alive for a long time in this way. As long as they're in meditation they're alive, not dead.

Therefore it's important that meditators try to change the laws in their country so that they can be left alone at the time of death; this is their human right. They need to get the government's permission for their body not to be disturbed until the signs that their consciousness has left their body have appeared.

Some lamas say that the clear light experience is an experience of emptiness. Others say that it's an artificial experience, not a real experience of emptiness. There's some debate about this. Those who say it's not real argue that since everybody goes through the clear light experience and not everybody can understand emptiness, it's merely a superficial experience of emptiness. Others disagree.

However, whether or not the clear light is a genuine experience of emptiness is not our business; we don't need to fight over or debate this point. It's good enough that we simply put a stop to our concrete conceptions and superstitions and experience nonduality or non-self-existence. As far as I'm concerned, that's the Swiss chocolate and we don't need to debate whether that's a true experience of emptiness or not.

Now, intellectually, we can discuss these issues among ourselves. I can ask you, "What is your experience of emptiness?" and you can reply, "At the time I experienced emptiness I saw no girlfriend, no boyfriend, no chocolate…." I can then debate back, "What! You have no problem with chocolate? That's not emptiness. You have no husband or wife problem, no political problem? That's your experience of emptiness? That can't be emptiness." I can try to convince you that what you describe is not the experience of emptiness.

But let's look at it from the practical point of view. To experience emptiness we have to build up to it gradually from our present complete lack of it. First we need a baby emptiness experience, then a teenage one, then a middle-age emptiness experience, then an elderly one, and finally the great emptiness experience. I'm talking about this from the practical point of view, not an intellectual one. Intellectually, some people think, "Emptiness is this, so when you have the experience it should be that." That's just an intellectual trip, not an organic, experiential one. The organic experience is where you start slowly, slowly, slowly, slowly, slowly and, as your · concrete concepts decrease, an experience of emptiness gradually builds up. It's slow and gradual—that's why an intellectual explanation of emptiness and the actual experience are very different.

When the clear light experience stops, signs that the mind has left the body appear. Female energy in the form of blood comes out of the nostrils and clear liquid male energy leaves the sexual organ. After that the visions reappear in reverse order. From the clear light we experience the black vision followed by the red and the white. Then all the superstitions arise once more. So now I'm talking about the intermediate state, the *bardo*. In other words, we go from the death of this life, the clear light, into the bardo body and experience the black, red and white visions in that order, and from there the ego is rebuilt once more.

If you are sensitive and aware you'll notice that emotions arising in the ignorant mind are associated with certain colors. Craving and desire have their own color; jealousy and hatred have theirs. You should try to be aware of that kind of vision.

Here I'm talking about experiences at the time of death, but we have similar ones when we go to sleep, faint or have an orgasm. We should be aware of all this. We've experienced death so many times but we've been unconscious, too insensitive to recognize what we're going through, uncomprehending of the experiences we've had.

So the death process is not an unusual thing; we've experienced

it many times, during orgasm and so forth, as I just mentioned—
the absorption of our elements, the mirage, smoke, sparks and
flickering candle appearances, the white, red, black and clear light
visions—but because of our heavy ignorance we've been unconscious of them. If we can be conscious and sensitive and maintain
intensive awareness of our actions, we will notice and understand
the death process whenever it occurs in our life. We've experienced
it frequently, not just since we started meditating.

All of us have had valuable experiences in the past. This doesn't
mean we're great meditators; everybody has experienced the death
process countless times. However, what's important is to acknowl-
edge, or be conscious, of the valuable experiences we've had and to
bring them to mind, to remember them. Doing so gives us confidence in our practice and helps our spiritual growth. What we're
doing at the moment, however, is unconsciously throwing all our
valuable experiences into the garbage. That's not right. We have all
these valuable inner experiences but we totally ignore them, throw
them away, and instead put on the concrete blanket of ignorance
and wear it everywhere. We discard precious, valuable experiences
that money can't buy and are integral parts of us, ignore them, and
put on what we're not and try to wear that around. It's completely
foolish.

Well, so much for that. Now I'd better get back to our main order
of business: OM AH HUM.

The OM AH HUM meditation

Visualize a white OM in the center of your brain. Recognize it as the pure energy of divine sound making the sound OM. It symbolizes the divine body of a buddha or bodhisattva or whatever else you consider to be pure. Then, when you say OM, much radiant white light streams from that syllable down your central channel, into your body, entirely purifying its impure energy and completely filling it from head to toe with blissful radiant white energy. Feel that strongly.

Now recite OMMM for two or three minutes. As you do, meditate that you're purifying your body. When you stop, hold your consciousness right there, without discriminating good or bad. Just be aware. Don't react, don't engage in any internal conversation, just focus with intensive awareness on the light permeating your body. Put your mind on that, keep it there and let go, without sluggishness or distraction.

Don't squeeze yourself into what you consider to be the right mediation posture. Just sit naturally, comfortably. Similarly, leave your neck in a comfortable position. Breathe naturally; let your energy flow naturally. Don't think, "I'm a meditator"; don't think, "I'm so humble"; don't think, "I'm such an egotist." Don't think anything at all. Just be.

Also, put your hands into whatever position is comfortable. They don't have to be held in any special way for you to attain single-pointed concentration. Just do whatever's comfortable.

Now close your eyes, visualize the white OM in the center of your brain making the sound *om*, and let's all chant OMMM together for a couple of minutes. As you chant, visualize much blissful radiant *kundalini* energy emanating from the OM, filling your entire body and purifying all your impure energy. It's important here to visualize your whole body full of radiant white light energy; everything is radiant white energy. It's important to see this. It helps break down your critical concepts of your body.

[Everybody chants OMMM together for two minutes.]

Good. Now rest in a state of intensive awareness … let go … without any expectation.

Your intensive awareness leads you to experience zero, egolessness, total emptiness, nothingness. Comprehend that with intensive awareness and let go.

All right. If we don't stop meditating now perhaps we'll lose ourselves. Thank you so much.

··· 5 ···

Understanding and Dealing with Death

Y ESTERDAY WE WERE talking about the many confusing things that can occur during the death process. And as you know, from the Buddhist point of view, confusion and disease come from the three poisons: desire, hatred and ignorance. So all the hallucinated visions we experience at death come from these three poisons. If we were free from them we'd have no problems at the time of death. It would be blissful.

This is important to know. When we describe the death process, with the absorption of the four elements and the resultant confusion, we're talking about people whose minds are occupied by the three poisons. The poisons are what cause imbalance of the body's elements. Saying that the elements absorb means that the elements get out of balance.

As I also mentioned, when you listen to teachings on this topic you'll hear things like "the elements absorb" or "earth sinks into water," which is the kind of language found in Tibetan texts on this subject. This is just terminology. There's no such thing as earth actually sinking into water, water sinking into fire and so forth. Scientifically speaking, one element deteriorates and disappears, causing bodily imbalance and mental confusion. Anyway, this deterioration and imbalance comes from the three poisons.

Those who have some familiarity with Tibetan medical terminology will have heard of *rlung*, usually in reference to a disturbance of the air element. When desire arises it produces strong air energy in your nervous system—the air doesn't move smoothly and there can be hyperventilation. Jealousy and hatred disturb the bile. Hatred especially produces too much fire, an excess of the fire element. Ignorance produces an excess of water. So when one of the three poisons is strong it causes its corresponding element to get strong. This creates an imbalance among the elements, causes confusion within us and can even lead to death.

Our air element is supposed to preserve our life but if it gets out of balance we can die. It's the same with our fire element: normally it sustains our life but if there's an explosion of heat it can kill us. What about water? Water is necessary, but again, if there's too much we can die. When our elements are correctly balanced, good things happen; when one gets way out of balance, we die. That's our reality.

Some of you might have read the *Bardo Thödrol* [*The Tibetan Book of the Dead*]. In it there are descriptions of the horrible visions some people have when they're dying, like being attacked by somebody with a knife and things like that. In one way, it looks kind of exaggerated: "How could that be?" It seems too much. Another way, however, I think it can be true, because we have accumulated so many layers of negativity—not just in this life but from beginningless previous lives, one piled on top of the other—that they ripen in this overwhelming way.

I heard on TV that there's a singer who's sold so many records that if you piled them up they would be higher than Mt. Everest. Our heavy blankets of confusion are just like that: if you piled them up they would be even higher than that...two or three times higher than Mt. Everest. So because of all these imprints of confusion it's possible that during the death process all kinds of visions can appear.

For example, we see people in hospital with terminal cancer suffering greatly, going in and out of consciousness—for me, that's like hell. When I see people in a cancer ward I don't need any other explanation of hell. Of course, we have detailed explanations of hell, but for me, the cancer ward's enough. It's not usual suffering; it's unusual, worse than animal suffering. Those patients are conscious, slip into unconsciousness and the death process, and then come to again. Have you seen people suffering like this? For me that's a hellish experience. So I'm going to say that this kind of situation is absolutely the same as that which the *Bardo Thödrol* describes: exaggerated visions of *yamas* with horns coming to eat you and things like that.

I was in San Francisco a few years ago and went to see some cancer patients. That night I couldn't sleep; seeing those people was too much for me. It was like hell.

That's why it's so important that you keep yourself clean clear all the time. Every day, keep yourself as clean clear as possible. Don't create confused situations with your body, speech or mind. It's simple. Then you'll have no problems. You'll be balanced both internally and externally and will also not be in danger of contracting a serious disease.

When you meditate and the negative forces of confusion enter your mind, recognize them for what they are: confusion, illusion and untruth. That will help you understand non-self-existence and nonduality when you're dying. You'll develop a more stable comprehension of reality and that will make a big difference as to whether or not you can cope with what's happening at the time of death. If the illusions that appear shake you too much, you'll have no control, but if, when the illusory appearances come, you have a strong mind, you'll be able to maintain control.

If you're seriously ill with advanced disease and tremendous confusion, you can't cope; you can't keep yourself clean clear because of the overwhelming power of your confusion. But if you die in a more normal way without tremendously heavy illness and confusion, you can cope with the death process by yourself and keep your consciousness clean clear. When the various stages of death occur you'll be able to explain to yourself, "Now this is happening, now that will come..." and watch what's going on almost as if were happening outside of yourself. What I'm saying is that being conscious and having control during the death process depends a lot on your mind's being free of the three poisons. That's the conclusion.

Perhaps you're thinking how is it possible for craving desire to arise at the time of death? Craving desire arises on the basis of fantasy. Our normal, everyday, waking-state life's craving desire is, of course, a fantasy, but even though when we are dying our eyes are closed and everything is shutting down, still, the experience of past fantasies can arise and cause us to grasp at our future coming life. This is similar to the way that craving desire can arise so strongly in our dreams that we ejaculate. Our dying body can be as cold as ice with no circulation but these kinds of things can be going on within our mind.

Fortunate people who die naturally, without heavy disease or confusion, have a very smooth death. The advantage they have is that of clean clear control. Even though some confusion might arise when their elements absorb, they can recognize the various appearances as hallucinations and understand that there's no self-existent earth, water, fire and so forth, and therefore maintain control. Then, slowly, slowly, as more elements absorb, they naturally become clearer and clearer and approach non-self-existent, or nondual, unification and are slowly led to the completely clear light stage. Instead of causing confusion, the death process allows such fortunate people to touch reality. Death can bring good things or bad; here I'm talking about some good things that can happen.

However, you shouldn't worry that death must be difficult and rebirth even worse; that you might be reborn in the lower realms as a tiger, a donkey, a monkey or something. I tell you, don't worry. Even though we might not have great wisdom, we do have a certain degree of loving kindness, and if we die with loving kindness in our mind we'll never have to worry about getting a bad rebirth. With loving kindness in your mind there's no way you'll be reborn in the lower realms.

The OM AH HUM meditation (continued)

Now we're going to do another short meditation. Last time we purified our body; now we're going to purify our speech. This means
purifying our uncontrolled negative speech, such as that which
harms others, telling lies, causing pain to others and so forth. That's
what I mean by negative speech.

Visualize a red AH at your throat chakra radiating red light energy,
like the sun at sunset. Recognize this red AH as the pure speech of all
the buddhas and bodhisattvas.

Light radiates from the AH and your whole body is embraced by
radiant red light energy, especially your throat chakra. At the same
time, recite AAAHHH for a couple of minutes. Then stop, just as we
did last time, and remain in a state of total intense awareness of your
own consciousness. Stay there without any expectation or interpretation of anything. Just be intensively aware. Stay there.

[Everybody recites AAAHHH . . . .]

When you experience the non-self-existent I, or nothingness, zero,
emptiness or space, understand that this is the truth, reality; this
gives strength to your comprehension of nonduality. Comprehend
this strongly. This experience is much more real than that of the
waking fantasy sense world.

If uncontrollable distracted thoughts arise, think that not only
you but all sentient beings as well are in the same uncontrolled situation and generate equilibrium and much loving-kindness toward

all others. In this way your uncontrolled mind becomes a resource for you to generate loving kindness. Contemplate on feeling loving-kindness for others. When loving-kindness arises, exert intensive awareness on the mind of loving-kindness.

So there are two things you're doing in this meditation. Either you're remaining in intensive awareness on your consciousness or, when distracted, exerting intensive awareness of the loving-kindness within your own mind. Alternate between these two.

Next, your loving-kindness manifests as a full moon in your heart chakra. At the center of the full moon is a blue HUM radiating blue light and making the sound of HUM. Recognize this as the nondual wisdom energy of all the buddhas and bodhisattvas. Your heart feels cool, calm and fully opened by the radiant light of the moon and the infinite radiant blue light coming from the HUM.

All narrow thoughts disappear.

All indecisive minds disappear.

All obsessed minds disappear.

Much light radiates from the moon and the blue HUM filling your entire body with infinite light energy and a feeling of great bliss.

Because you are totally embraced by the infinite blue light, there's no room for fanatical dualistic concepts.

Now for a couple of minutes we're going to recite HUM together. Then feel that the infinite blue light pervades your consciousness and that your consciousness and intensive awareness embrace the entire scope of universal reality. Feel this, be this, without any expectation or superstition whatsoever.

(Everybody recites HUUUMMM together for two minutes.)

So, we need two experiences: wisdom and method. The first is the experience of penetrative wisdom, intensive awareness of the reality of your own consciousness. That's the way to approach wisdom. Method comes in when you lose control over your mind and get completely distracted. That experience of distraction becomes a resource for you to generate loving-kindness. In other words, distraction does not become that much of a problem because you use it to generate loving-kindness. Once you're free of distraction, return to abiding in wisdom. So your business is dual: wisdom and loving-kindness. No problem, go into wisdom; problem, loving-kindness. So, in addition to your day job, you have these two other orders of business.

Then, the OM AH HUM mantra is very useful. You people are very busy, so if you do not have time to recite long mantras you can simply recite OM AH HUM. It represents all mantras. Especially when you say OMMM, your intensive awareness consciousness is energized to awaken.

Recently somebody told me about some scientists who found in their experiments that sound is restorative for the brain. They discovered that mantra activates awakening in the brain, makes it function rather than sleep. Not so many people understand this, not even scientists. So when you say OMMM your entire nervous system is energized.

That's what meditation means: awakening from sleep. Here it means you awaken to broad reality rather than your usual fanatic reality, you touch universal reality in a kind of way. That's why mantra is very useful.

Conclusion

It seems that we're out of time but I'm satisfied that I've dealt with the subject I was supposed to talk about adequately. The important thing is to convince yourself clean clear, not just intellectually but through your own experience of meditation, that you can to some extent remain in intensive awareness of your own consciousness without distraction or sluggishness. That's good enough. And the important thing here is that in Buddhism, intensive awareness of your own consciousness is like a nuclear missile—a missile to penetrate the nonduality of space. It's very important that you understand this.

It means that there's no "this way, that way." When you focus completely on awareness of your own consciousness, I can guarantee that this internal nuclear missile will enter the space of nonduality and that's what you'll experience. At that time, when you experience nonduality, or emptiness, you need to build up the strength of your intensive awareness comprehending that this is reality and not allow any internal "that this" conversation. You need to strengthen your internal understanding that nonduality is what's real.

Why is it necessary to strengthen your comprehension or awareness of the nonduality of your own consciousness? It's because normally we think fantasy is real and grasp at it. Then, when we have an experience of nonduality, because it's the opposite of what we've always believed to be real we tend to think, "Oh, this is not true." Since our habit is to see fantasy as concrete, when we have an inner experience we think it's not real. Therefore we need to strengthen our understanding that inner experiences *are* real.

I think that's enough. I'm afraid I haven't had time to go into the details of the intermediate state and how from there we proceed into the next life. It's complicated and would take much time to explain.[4]

---

[4] See *The Great Treatise on the Stages of the Path to Enlightenment, Volume One*, pp. 307–313.

The main thing, however, is to gain inner experiences. Then you will see how it's possible to go into the bardo and reincarnate and you won't need to listen to my "blah, blah, blah" on these topics. You'll discover the truth through your own experience.

I think we have time for a couple of questions, just to make sure I haven't created too much difficulty or confusion for you.

Q. How can we help a dying person?

Lama. It depends on the person's religious background, training and philosophy. Whatever it is, you need to do something to energize or wake the person up accordingly. The most important thing is not to irritate the person; leave him alone. When you feel he's ready to go, leave him alone. Don't say, "Take some medicine" or "Sign here"; don't cry: "Oh…you're going to die…." That makes it very difficult.

For example, say I'm your father and I'm dying. You come in crying, "Oh, Daddy, you're dying. How can I live without you?" I get terribly disturbed and can't cope with the situation. So it's better to just let go. Don't make the dying person tremendously anxious or emotionally disturbed. Just leave him in peace. That's very important.

Instead, try to give the person confidence. "OK, you're dying, but everything's all right. Be happy; don't worry. Now is the perfect time to go." Try to help in this way. Also, the environment is important. Make sure there's nothing in it likely to increase the person's attachment or hatred. Make sure the situation is very quiet and peaceful.

If the person's a Christian you can say, "God will take care of you. You're lucky, you're going to heaven." Be positive. It's good, because at that moment, even if she wasn't that much of a Christian during her life, inside, subconsciously, she's looking for some opportunity at that moment. Because she has nothing, she's looking for something to hang on to, to take refuge in. So when we mention God or Jesus, we touch the person's subconscious. That's very good. In my opinion, it's possible. Many Europeans say that they have nothing to do with their country's religion but still, it has had a lot to do with their life or mentality. Subconsciously, they're Christian. On the conscious level they might say, "I don't want to be a Christian" and when they get into a disastrous or critical situation they have nothing to hang on to. So if you mention God or Jesus, there's something for them to grasp. That's very useful. Then, of course, if the person's a Buddhist you can mention the Buddha.

Q. What happens to a confused mental patient who's always saying, "I'm going to hell," and dies still saying it?
Lama. It can happen. In a way, some people can already be halfway to hell. They can see it coming. Intellectually, it's very difficult to help such people; at that moment it's a hopeless situation. It might be possible to help them medically, kind of slow them down and ease their confusion, but otherwise it's very difficult.

Q. Zen Buddhism has koans to help us understand non-inherent existence. How does "What is the sound of one hand clapping," for example, relate to shunyata? How would meditating on that help us realize shunyata?
Lama. Our fantasy concrete concepts hold things to be self-existent,

like the self-existent husband and self-existent wife I mentioned before, or the Swiss government believing that only the self-existent Swiss franc can make a perfect self-existent Swiss society.

All this self-existent fantasy that we hold as real does not touch reality. To make a sound, your two hands have to touch each other. Similarly, to touch reality you first have to discover that holding on to all your fantasies, concepts and preconceptions is like trying to make sound by clapping with one hand and finding there's no sound. Then the zero of the sound, the zero of the self-existent fantasy, disappears. This is the way to experience shunyata.

Also, here, OMMM... the sound OM is an interdependent phenomenon. It's interdependent with my entire nervous system. There's no self-existent OM sound, is there? There's no self-existent sound at all. Sound depends on the voice box, space, energy and many other things. Every sound is completely interdependent—many factors have to cooperate together to produce sound. So sound itself demonstrates the nature of non-self-existence.

Buddhism often uses sound to explain non-self-existence or nonduality. One example is that of an echo, where you shout toward a rock cliff and the sound bounces back. That's a good example. Sound is a perfect example of the character of interdependence. The factors in its production totally depend upon each other. Understanding the character of interdependence is evidence that there's no concrete, self-existent I or self-existent anything else.

If you hold sound to be self-existent, then it would not be dependent on two hands striking each other. That's the rational Buddhist scientific explanation. If sound were self-existent it would not

depend on two hands coming together and would not be an interdependent phenomenon.

So I think we now have a good understanding of interdependent
phenomena. Our gathering together here is also a non-self-existent
phenomenon.

Thank you very much, everybody, especially those who invited me
to Switzerland to conduct this seminar and put so much effort into
making these excellent arrangements. I dedicate your hard work
to be of benefit to all sentient beings, so let's all dedicate like that
together.

And since my talks have no doubt produced a lot of confusion,
as long as I'm still here on earth, you know my address, so you can
write me and I will answer. I'm responsible for what I've been talking about and for cleaning up my own garbage. So you can write
me; I'm not going to disappear immediately.[5]

---

[5] However, less than six months later Lama did, in fact, disappear from sight. This
was his last teaching in the West and second-last ever. He passed away in Los Angeles
3 March 1984.

Transference of Consciousness

Lama Yeshe

London, 1982

···6···
Transference of Consciousness

TONIGHT I'M SUPPOSED to talk about the Himalayan yogic experience of transference of consciousness [Tib: *powa*]. Well, as it happens, the last time I was in the Himalayas I interviewed a mountain yogi about his experiences of this practice....

No, actually, this method of transferring the consciousness comes from the teachings of Shakyamuni Buddha. It's not the fabrication of some Tibetan monks. It was given by Shakyamuni, passed down through the oral transmission lineage, came to Tibet, and is now part of the Tibetan tradition.

Who has to practice the transference of consciousness and what are its benefits?

First of all, from the Buddhist point of view, human life and death are equally important events. There's no reason to think that life is important and death is bad, unimportant. You should not think that way. Both are important.

We all want a happy life, don't we? Himalayan yogis, however, prefer a happy death. They don't want a death that's disastrous, unhappy or confused.

Of course, those who have attained enlightenment in their lifetime don't need to transfer their consciousness, but those who have not and have to take another life do need to do so. Certain overwhelming conditions, such as serious disease or wrong thinking, grasping and attachment, create a disastrous situation at the time of death and can prevent yogis from dying a perfect death, so yogis practice the methods for transferring the consciousness before such conditions arise.

Because of karma, the life force or whatever other reason, we seem to be stuck in our sense gravitation attachment body with no way out, but yogis train in such a way that they facilitate the transfer of their consciousness out of their sense gravitation body and free themselves from fear and a disastrous death. So when they feel they are free, that the time is right for them to transfer their consciousness, they can do it by applying the appropriate technical meditation.

I'm not just talking philosophy here. Many Tibetan monks and meditators have utilized these techniques when the time has been right. For example, I heard that after the Chinese conquered Tibet in 1959, many ordinary monks employed these methods to happily leave this life because they felt they no longer had the right to exercise their religious faith. This is a true fact. Therefore it's very useful to have this kind of experience.

It's important for Westerners to know about this because up until now you've largely neglected conscious phenomena and the ability to use your mind meaningfully and instead have busied yourselves with material things. So it's a good thing to introduce the idea that you have the power to eliminate disastrous life situations by eradicating the fear of death, fear of life and sense gravitation attachment. Anybody can do this because all people have buddha potential. It exists within all of us, so we should not feel that we're stuck and can't do anything about it. We have the ability to free ourselves from all confusion and suffering.

It's important to recognize that the primary resource of all happiness, misery, fear and confusion is the mind, not the physical body, but to fully understand our mind we need to investigate it. Understanding the nature of our mind is also the path to freedom from all fear.

We have to choose the right time to transfer our consciousness; we're not allowed to do it at the wrong time because that becomes suicide. So we have specific times and scientifically determined signals of impending death that indicate when it's appropriate to engage in powa; there are detailed explanations of the internal and external signs that arise to show that death may be near. But it's also possible to change that situation.

We already know that to a certain extent we can change any circumstance, including a shortage of life energy. Life is an energy force; when it dwindles we can reactivate it in our nervous system. We have methods for extending life and postponing the onset of death but I'm not going to detail them here; this is simply an introductory talk.

So why transfer the consciousness? Death is coming; natural transference of consciousness is coming anyway, so why employ these methods? The reason is that we usually die because of illness, and if it's too advanced it overwhelms us and we can't cope.

So before our disease has progressed to that point, while we're still in relatively good condition, we transfer our consciousness at that time. Otherwise it's like committing suicide. So we should not practice powa without a proper understanding of the signs and signals of impending death, but when we reach a certain point where we're clean clear still in control, we use it then.

What's the way to do powa? Basically it's a matter of putting our concentration and energy into the right channel and preventing it from going the wrong way. Of course, there's extremely detailed technical information about how to do this.

What I mean by going the wrong way is the consciousness leaving the body via the wrong orifice, like the mouth, nose, navel or lower orifices. The Buddha's teachings explain in great detail the different kinds of rebirth we get if our mind leaves the body through one of those doors.

The point is, therefore, to have our consciousness leave through the crown of our head. If we can open this door and consciously, deliberately, mindfully separate our mind from our body through it, we give ourselves the ability to choose our next rebirth the best way and then continuously go from happy life to happy life. That's the main point.

One important thing to note is that even though you might have been a good, kind, loving person your whole life, if, at the time of death, you can't cope and perhaps die angry, you destroy everything positive you did your whole life.

That's why we call transference of consciousness a super method. Even a person who has done incredibly negative things—for example, Hitler, who killed millions of human beings and created unbelievably negative karma—can say goodbye to all his negativity if he uses this method perfectly at the time of death and dies with a clean clear mind. Since death really is a kind of final destination, we have to make sure we're clean clear at that time. If we can, that's our insurance for a perfect next life.

However, Himalayan practitioners have to prepare before they engage in powa. They practice the techniques and also make sure that they have no attachment to even a single material atom, that there's not one single object they grasp at. That's the most important thing.

What interferes with a good death, what makes you fearful, is the grasping mind. Any object that causes grasping attachment to arise while you're dying becomes a source of confusion and leads to a bad next life.

Some Westerners don't like to hear about rebirth but most people feel that something happens after death, whether you call it rebirth or not. That's good enough. Whether you say rebirth exists or not, as long as you feel from your heart or even intellectually that something continues beyond this life, that's good enough.

Traditionally, Tibetans who are going to die soon give all their possessions away so that at the time of death they own nothing. That's fantastic. When I was a young, inexperienced monk, seeing the older ones give everything away and die perfectly helped me a lot. It gave me confidence. Of course, we can all understand this intellectually, but to actually see others doing it makes you feel you can do it yourself. That's very important.

Also, we say that we transfer our consciousness to a pure land. From the Buddhist point of view, a pure land is not some place out there waiting for you. Pure means it's a reflection of your own pure thought, you own pure, clean clear mind. That's what we mean by pure land. Any environmental manifestation, good or bad, comes from the mind; it does not truly exist externally, from its own side, out there.

Normally, as we know, we like to project good things, but somehow, uncontrollably, bad projections come. Check it out. To project good things it's important to be positive and happy, but not in an overestimated way. You can have good projections of other human beings in a realistic way. This is important. People appear the way you want them to. If you want to see them in a bad light, that's how they'll appear to you. Visions of good and bad come from you, not external objects.

This means that, with respect to our visions and concepts, we have a choice. We also have the capacity to augment that view, whether it's positive or negative. Since we have a choice, we should always choose the good one.

However, we have technical meditations to retain and increase the life-force energy that leaves our body through the various orifices at the time of death. These meditations help us keep that energy in and thus extend our lifespan. Remember, life depends on the movement of the breath.

How many breaths do you take in twenty-four hours? Does the West have a count? Buddhism does.

What we do is examine our breathing. If the breath is uneven, coming out more strongly from one nostril than the other, that can be a sign of approaching death. Those are warning signals, if you're aware. If you investigate and notice this imbalance you can change the rhythm of your breath and extend your life through meditation.

Also, transference of consciousness isn't done by the mind alone. When training ourselves to transfer our consciousness we also use the energy force of the movement of the physical breath by using certain techniques of meditating on the breath. Practicing these meditations also involves concentration on the chakras, such as those at the heart and navel. Meditating at these points brings different realizations and experiences. In other words, Tibetan Buddhism employs physical resources, not just mental ones.

Recent scientific research has mentioned pleasure centers and chemicals in the brain. Similarly, Tibetan Buddhist tantra also talks about a bliss, or happiness, center. If we concentrate there we activate its energy and produce a blissful experience. For that reason, when we meditate on transference of consciousness, the technique focuses on different chakras. And success in this produces various signs, such as the generation of heat, improved digestion and so forth. Also, you feel as if you are no longer stuck in sense gravitation attachment and that somehow you have transcended mundane life. We should develop our life, enjoy our life. That means utilizing our innate resources to go beyond our normal bondage and inertia.

Of course, many people are scared of death because first, they think it's going to be a disaster, with much difficulty and suffering, and second, they believe that after death they're going into great misery. Their projection and presumption is that this is what's going to happen. In order to stop that worry—even if you can't transfer your consciousness—if you can lessen your self-cherishing and attachment to your own body and position and increase your loving-kindness for others, that's absolutely good enough to alleviate fear of death and the next life and guarantee yourself a good rebirth. A dedicated attitude itself is peaceful, so this is the way to ensure a good death and freedom from worry of a bad rebirth—even if you can't transfer your consciousness.

Not only can your consciousness transfer to a pure land; it can also go into another body. The mind is really powerful. Through meditation and concentration you can heat or move objects. Through the power of your mind you can also eliminate emotional disturbance—attachment, confusion and so forth, which is actually the main point of practicing Dharma. In other words, you can completely change your mind; you can change your misery into happiness.

However, the question is, do you really want to or not? Are you truly seeking or not? If you are a true seeker, you know intuitively that you can do something. That's the power of the human mind. Don't make limited judgments of yourself. We all have good thoughts, positive thoughts, which can be developed infinitely. That's the beauty of human consciousness; it has limitless potential. We all have a little loving-kindness—that small amount of loving-kindness can be developed into infinite loving-kindness.

The nature of loving-kindness is peace and happiness. The nature of self-cherishing and attachment is misery and confusion. So, to have an easygoing and happy life you have to be willing to correct your attitude, believe that you can indeed do it, and be prepared to put in the effort required. A weak mind eliminates all potentiality.

The reason we feel trapped is because we're so attached to our body. We pretty much identify our body as "me." The true fact, however, is that your body is *not* you. Your bones are not you. Your real essence is your consciousness, which has neither shape nor color. It's a materialistic attitude that thinks, "I'm the body." That's fundamentally wrong thinking. "I am my body" becomes "My body is nice, so I'm nice; my body is ugly, so I'm ugly; my body is happy, so I'm happy." That's the wrong attitude. Somebody can be slicing chunks of flesh off your body but your mind can be blissful, peaceful and tranquil. It's possible. That's the point. Your body can be sick but your mind can be completely radiant and blissful. So my point is that you should abandon all concepts of "My body is me."

Most Westerners don't understand the difference between the body and the mind. You need to. That's why you find it difficult to see that there's life after death. Believing that your body is you, when your body gives out you're left thinking, "How can I go on? Where am I?"

The thing is that Buddhism is not saying that you exist permanently or that the you of this life goes on unchanged to the next. When Buddhism talks about rebirth it's saying that your consciousness changes shape, takes another body. Why? Because anyway, you're constantly grasping at something, so when your relationship with this body finishes you naturally grasp at something else. At that point your consciousness takes another body and that's the reason Buddhism calls it rebirth. Rebirth doesn't mean taking this body into your next life.

The basic understanding is that after you die your consciousness continues and carries your experiences with you. If you understand this, you can relax. You don't have to make yourself completely busy: "This twentieth century life, I have to do everything; I have to experience everything in this life." There are so many trips on this earth that you can take. "I want to do this, I want to do that...I want to do the monkey trip, I want to do the chicken trip, I want to do the pig trip...I have to do them now, otherwise I'll miss out. I have only one life." That's not true—you'll have many future lives, so there's no need to rush.

By understanding the power of the mind you find a way to satisfy yourself. That's very important for all of us. We have to find a way of satisfying ourselves, of making our life content, rather than living with the feeling that life is empty and worthless. You should feel that your life is the most precious thing, more precious than all the money in the world.

So, knowing the characteristic nature of your own consciousness is how you bring peace into yourself and the world in general, because it comes to you through your own experience. Peace is your own experience, not something external. The beauty of peace is something that has to be experienced, and with peace comes satisfaction. It has to be generated within you and once it has, you can give it to others. Then you can truly bring peace to the world. Before bringing peace to others and the world, you first have to experience it yourself. The opposite of peace is grasping; the grasping mind is the opposite of peace. You can see this within yourself and in the world around you.

However, rather than continuing to talk it might be better if I were to answer some questions.

Q. What should we do in the case of sudden death, such as in an accident?

Lama. That's difficult to say. It depends on time and space. If there's no time or space to set up your mind, then you just have to let go. That's just the way it is. But if there is time and space, like you know the accident's going to happen, you can set your mind up in the right way. Instead of being afraid you can concentrate your mind, or if you have time to transfer your consciousness you can do that. It depends on time and space.

Q. What if we die unconscious or, as often happens in the West, heavily drugged or sedated in hospital?

Lama. If you're unconscious, let go. You can't change that, unless it's a situation where a drug will restore consciousness. If one can't communicate with a dying person's intellect, there's not much can be done.

Q. Lama, could you please describe consciousness, and do you distinguish between the ego-consciousness and the unconscious?

Lama. Consciousness is a kind of clear energy that takes the reflection of all existent phenomena, even though it doesn't have form or color itself. Ego-consciousness is consciousness but has to be eradicated. From the Buddhist point of view, ego-consciousness is negative, a negative aspect of consciousness that gradually has to be abandoned. But you don't need to get rid of the general conscious-ness, which continues from life to life. Within it are both positive and negative consciousnesses. The positive continues and doesn't need to be abandoned. It's the negative, or ego-consciousness, that has to be eradicated, because it is the source of all conflict and con-fusion; the ego has to be abandoned.

Q. How can we help someone who is dying but has no knowledge of or contact with Dharma, to make that person's death easier?

Lama. If you know the dying person's history—lifestyle, faith, reli-gion, beliefs and so forth—you can try to bring it into the process. That's a good way to help. But whether the person's religious or not, you must make sure that the environment is peaceful and tranquil and not make the person angry or agitated. Leave the person alone; don't show "You're dying; I'm in pain." Let the person go happily. That's very important.

Q. Could you say something about the transference of conscious-ness that takes place at birth, if it does, and can we assist the one being born in this process?

Lama. It's possible to choose your rebirth, to have a choice. Some-how you think about the kind of perfect view and concepts you would like, maintain the continuity of that perfect view, and even-tually it leads you to that kind of situation. Does that make sense?

First of all, you should understand that because of the continuity of consciousness, there's actually never either death or rebirth. What we call "death" and "rebirth" are artificial—momentary, relative changes of shape, that's all. You simply change your conventional form but your real mind—that which you've had from the time you were born and will continue after you die—goes on without a break.

In other words, you take your experiences with you. From the Buddhist point of view, your mind contains not only this life's experiences—you carry with you countless lives' experiences. That's what we call karma. And since grasping at something to hang on to is inherent within you—it's in the nature of the ego to grasp; it can't exist without grasping at something—after the death of this life, when the force connecting your mind to your body disappears, you still seek something to hang on to. That's the reason rebirth occurs: because of grasping.

But if you're clean clear and die in a liberated way, you don't need to worry; you can choose to have perfect happiness in your next life. There's nothing to worry about. But if at the time of death you're confused and tremendously fearful, that will bring you a different kind of life. It's decided at the time of death.

Q. As bodhisattvas, should we allow the bodhicitta to choose our future rebirth or should we try to obtain liberation from cyclic existence altogether?

Lama. Bodhisattvas are dedicated more to the safety, happiness and liberation of others than their own. Their duty is to lead others to perfection and not be concerned with their own liberation. A dying bodhisattva prays to realize bodhicitta in her next life, not to quickly gain personal liberation and go somewhere pleasant herself. That would be selfish, wouldn't it? Anyway, seeking your own liberation can sometimes bring much misery and disappointment. Dedicating yourself to others gives you time and space so that you don't suffocate. Sometimes people who meditate for their own liberation become very uptight.

Q. How much is love of an individual person attachment? Does it prevent the state of mind necessary for the transference of consciousness?

Lama. That depends. Having a human relationship doesn't necessarily mean building up attachment and grasping. If you have that kind of relationship then yes, it does become an obstacle to freeing your mind.

Q. Why is there such suffering in relationships between men and women these days? What is the meaning of this? And what will help us face and live with this?

Lama. It's simple. First of all, twentieth century people have too much superstition, too much freedom to exercise their ego, and this spills over into their relationships, which tend to be too strong, too extreme and too superficial, the result of which is conflict and dissatisfaction. So that's my answer: if human relationships are superficial and extreme, the result is conflict. They're not realistic. You can't make the vase and flowers one. Intellectually, people in extreme relationships want to make two people one; there's too much expectation of making two into one—it's not possible. In other words, you can't make two egos one. You need to make time and space for another ego. Also, from the Buddhist point of view, we each have our own individual concepts and elements of mind, so we need to allow the freedom for these to be exercised. Even though you feel this person is your dear friend, he or she can't become one with you—unless you both discover the absolute truth.

Q. How can we keep our minds clear and happy with so much suffering around us?

Lama. That question's just an excuse! What you're saying is, "I'm unhappy and dissatisfied because so many other people are unhappy and dissatisfied." That's not logical. You're responsible for your own happiness; you're responsible for your own satisfaction; you're responsible for your own misery.

Of course, you can't be careless of others' suffering. You have to be sympathetic. But a mind that has sympathy for others brings more satisfaction than misery. I want you to understand this. Some people have the misconception "How can I be satisfied while so many others are hungry and dissatisfied?" That's wrong thinking. If you have sympathy, love and compassion for all these people, that will bring you more satisfaction, but normally we react to others' suffering with emotion; we get emotionally disturbed. That's not really compassion; that's just an emotional reaction based on a misunderstanding of the situation. A correct understanding of the situation produces loving-kindness and the result of that is more happiness and joy, rather than misery.

So your question indicates faulty logic. Many people ask this kind of thing; I think it's wrong thinking. For example, you can say, "How can people in the world live in peace while there's war, killing and bloodshed in the Middle-East?" In my opinion, that's the wrong question.

Of course, we can say, "How can I be happy while there's so much misery in the world?" Relatively speaking you can ask this question, but scientifically, it's wrong. You can be satisfied and content even though others aren't. For example, Shakyamuni Buddha renounced the confusion of samsara, acted appropriately and achieved the enlightened experience. That was due to his own great effort in personal development. In the meantime, we're still here with our limited compassion and limited thinking. So it's completely up to the individual. If you act for peace, you get peace; if you put yourself onto the path to misery, you end up miserable.

But all that does not mean you should not have sympathy for others. Sympathy for others brings you satisfaction and happiness, not misery.

Q. You said that peace is the opposite of grasping. Would it be accurate to say that peace is being content with what occurs? Just accepting pain or pleasure or whatever happens with patience and equilibrium? Is this what brings peace and security?

Lama. I'm not sure about that. Acceptance is OK but it depends on how you accept. If you have the attitude, "Whatever comes, comes; I can't do anything," that's the wrong attitude. That's weak, because you then accept anything that comes along.

Wise acceptance is like, say you've broken your nose: it's already broken, the situation is there, so it's better to accept it. But it's wrong to decide to accept everything that comes along no matter what.

Actually, you do have the capacity to change the situation and direct it in whichever way you want it to go. Since you have the free will to change things, you should also have the discriminating wisdom that can judge, "I'll accept certain things that come along but others, I have to change." I think so.

You see, some religious people tend to believe too much: "God gives me my experiences; I have to accept everything"; "Everything comes from karma; I can't change anything"; "Today I'm hungry; I have to accept my hunger." That's all wrong. You can change the situation. That's the beauty of our lives. I tell you, you can definitely change any situation. That's the power of the human being. You can call it buddha nature, human nature or whatever.

So it's very important that we all recognize that we can deal with, transform, any difficult thought that arises. That's the power of the human being and that's why we say human life is so great. Animals can't do these things. We're not more fortunate than animals because we can accumulate much wealth. That's wrong. Some animals can be richer than human beings.

Q. Christ said, "Love thy neighbor." What does love mean to you?
Lama. Well, I think Jesus was very practical. He taught us to be less self-cherishing, love others and be more dedicated to their happiness than our own. If you're always mean and angry, irritating your family and colleagues, uptight with no love around you, saying

things like, "I love everybody in the world, I'm dedicated to every-body in the world" but when a thirsty person asks you for a drink of water, you say "Go away and leave me alone," that makes no sense.

That's why I say Jesus was very practical. Loving-kindness means we have to start with those around us. Actually, we have to start with ourselves. First we have to love and value ourselves. From there, from seeing our own good qualities, we can slowly, slowly develop love for others. If you're angry with yourself, for sure you're going to be angry with others. That's just scientific psychology. For that reason, be practical too. Surround yourself with love. That's so practical.

This is a very important question, actually. You can see, if com-panions—husband and wife, boyfriend and girlfriend—don't love each other yet have to stay together, it's a real disaster. Because you lose faith in each other you lose faith in other human beings. You disrespect your companion, you have a bad opinion of yourself, you have a bad opinion of your companion—how can you have a good opinion of others? You lose your inner dignity.

So, when practicing loving-kindness, it's best to start wherever you are, close to yourself. In that way it's realistic. You can't go to Africa every day, saying, "I love African people; I want to serve them." You can't bring breakfast to all Africans. You're better off making breakfast for your husband or your wife.

Q. Must I love and honor my parents? I find this very difficult.
Lama. From the Buddhist point of view, your parents have taken care of you for all the years since you were in your mother's womb, and

when you think about that kindness you create space to love them. Don't you find any parental kindness to think about? Don't you feel your parents' kindness in your life? If not, that's wrong. First of all, you say you have parents, so there must have been a period of time when they took care of you and held you dear. Also, look at how the many parents we see around us take care of their children. It's incredible. When I see how parents take care of their children twenty-four hours a day I feel like such a selfish monk! Mothers don't get a good night's sleep, not just for a day or two but for months, even years. That's too much.

So if you think about the situation positively you can always find much kindness in what your parents did for you. But, as I said before, if you generate a negative projection, everything, the whole world, appears negative to you. So if you think about your parents negatively, of course they will appear negative to you.

People who hate their parents are very peculiar. Their parents cared for them for years and they hate them but they can profess love for somebody they've met only recently and have known for just a few days. They think this new boyfriend or girlfriend is very kind but don't care about the people who took care of them for years and to whom they're very strongly karmically linked. Scientifically speaking, that's just wrong. You say "I love you" to somebody you've just met and to whom you're momentarily attracted and whose touch you crave, but you reject your parents, who have shown you love for many years. That's unreasonable—psychologically sick and scientifically incorrect. Unfortunately.

Also, it's dangerous. It shows that you don't understand your own life. It diminishes loving-kindness in the world. Anyway, whatever pleasure you experience comes from other people. Your body comes from your father and mother, your clothes come from the people who made them, your food derives from the effort of others...every pleasure comes from other people. Therefore, people are the kindest of beings. Since any pleasure you can think of comes from others, you should always dedicate to others.

Q. Is transference of consciousness something that anybody can learn as a specific technique or to do you have to practice it in isolated meditation all your life in order to be able to do it?
Lama. Anybody can learn this technique. It's quite easy. You don't have to go into a cave. Also, this kind of training is not just meditation. It has a scientific basis. We also use some physical force. Therefore it's something everybody can understand and utilize. But tonight, let's not transfer our consciousness but enjoy ourselves here instead!

Q. If you choose your rebirth badly, would abortion be a happy release and therefore not create negative karma for the mother?
Lama. It's definitely negative but still not certain. It depends on what the mother's situation becomes if she has the child. If going ahead with the pregnancy leads both of them to great suffering—for example, they both die—then it might be sensible to have an abortion. But if the child is aborted out of self-cherishing, that's heavy karma.

Nevertheless, heavy karma can still be completely purified; you can change it. It's not something absolutely unchangeable. That's the beauty of it. You can obliterate any kind of negative energy. You should not think, "I created bad karma; my life is over. The rest of my life's going to be a disaster." That's wrong. You do good things and bad things in your life—the good and the bad are more or less equal. That's OK. It's all just energy. Whatever actions you do, good or bad, it's all just energy. What matters is which is stronger, the positive or the negative. As your positive energy increases, your negative energy automatically decreases; if your negative energy increases too much, the positive has no power. However, you can increase your karmic energy or you can get rid of it altogether. This is the way it works; it's a natural thing.

Negativities are conventional reality: relative, changeable, transitory. That's their beauty. It doesn't matter what negativities you've created, you have the potential to overcome them. There's no need to go around thinking, "I created bad karma; I should feel guilty the rest of my life." That's wrong thinking. It means you're holding a permanent concept of negativity. There's no such thing as permanently existent negativity.

Remember the four noble truths? The first is true suffering and the first characteristic of that is impermanence. True suffering, any kind of suffering, is transitory and impermanent and its nature is empty, nondual. But if you then conceptualize, "This suffering situation is the worst thing in my life; I'm always going to suffer but I deserve it," if you beat yourself up like that, that's completely wrong. Of course, it could be like that if there were no solution but everything has a solution. Every negative action has an antidote that can make it vanish. Therefore you should not hold a permanent conception of any negativity. That's the basis of the method the Buddha taught: you can enter the spiritual path in this life and in this life attain enlightenment—in this life, in one life. That shows that you have the power or capacity to eliminate all negative energy and be free from all ego concepts and dualistic thought.

So, if there are no more questions, I'd like to thank you so much. I'm sorry tonight was rather general but I don't think this is the right time or place to detail the meditation techniques for transferring the consciousness. However, the reason I chose this topic to speak on is that somehow Westerners need to understand these concepts and in that way you can do something with your life. That's my main point.

It doesn't mean that you're going to become a great yogi or a great meditator. I don't care about that. But you can do something with your life, something with your mind, to keep your mind happy throughout your life. That's the most important thing for all of us. We all want to be happy for the rest of our life. We all want to be liberated from miserable situations and be able to deal with whatever comes up from moment to moment in our life. Buddhism teaches us how to do it.

References and Suggested
Further Reading

Gehlek Rimpoche. *Good Life, Good Death*. New York: Riverhead Books, 2001.

Gyatso, Tenzin, His Holiness the Dalai Lama. *The Joy of Living and Dying in Peace*. Translated by Donald S. Lopez Jr. San Francisco: HarperSanFrancisco, 1997. (Especially Chapter 2, "Dying in Peace.")

———. *Mind of Clear Light: Advice on Living Well and Dying Consciously*. Translated by Jeffrey Hopkins. New York: Atria Books, 2004.

Lati Rinbochay & Jeffrey Hopkins. *Death, Intermediate State and Rebirth*. Ithaca, NY: Snow Lion Publications, 1980.

Padmasambhava. *The Tibetan Book of the Dead*. Revealed by Terton Karma Lingpa, translated by Gyurme Dorje, edited by Graham Coleman and Thupten Jinpa, introduced by HH the Dalai Lama. London: Viking, 2006.

Pabongka Rinpoche. *Liberation in the Palm of Your Hand*. Translated by Michael Richards. Boston: Wisdom Publications, 1991. (Especially Day 10, "Remembering Death.")

Ribush, Nicholas. *Discovering Buddhism at Home, Module Five: Death and Rebirth*. Portland: FPMT, 2004.

Tsongkhapa. *The Great Treatise on the Stages of the Path to Enlightenment, Volume One*. The Lamrim Chenmo Translation Committee. Ithaca, NY: Snow Lion Publications, 2000. (Especially Chapter 9, "Mindfulness of Death.")

Zopa Rinpoche, Lama Thubten. *Heart Advice for Death and Dying*. Portland: FPMT, 2009. (Book and CD.)

Zopa Rinpoche, Lama Thubten & Kathleen McDonald. *Wholesome Fear: Transforming Your Anxiety about Impermanence and Death*. Boston: Wisdom Publications, 2010.

LAMA YESHE WISDOM ARCHIVE

The LAMA YESHE WISDOM ARCHIVE (LYWA) is the collected works of Lama Thubten Yeshe and Lama Thubten Zopa Rinpoche. Lama Zopa Rinpoche, its spiritual director, founded the ARCHIVE in 1996.

Lama Yeshe and Lama Zopa Rinpoche began teaching at Kopan Monastery, Nepal, in 1970. Since then, their teachings have been recorded and transcribed. At present we have well over 10,000 hours of digital audio and some 70,000 pages of raw transcript. Many recordings, mostly teachings by Lama Zopa Rinpoche, remain to be transcribed, and as Rinpoche continues to teach, the number of recordings in the ARCHIVE increases accordingly. Most of our transcripts have been neither checked nor edited.

Here at the LYWA we are making every effort to organize the transcription of that which has not yet been transcribed, edit that which has not yet been edited, and generally do the many other tasks detailed below.

The work of the LAMA YESHE WISDOM ARCHIVE falls into two categories: archiving and dissemination.

Archiving requires managing the recordings of teachings by Lama Yeshe and Lama Zopa Rinpoche that have already been collected, collecting recordings of teachings given but not yet sent to the ARCHIVE, and collecting recordings of Lama Zopa's on-going teachings, talks, advice and so forth as he travels the world for the benefit of all. Incoming media are then catalogued and stored safely while being kept accessible for further work.

We organize the transcription of audio, add the transcripts to the already existent database of teachings, manage this database, have transcripts checked, and make transcripts available to editors or others doing research on or practicing these teachings.

Other archiving activities include working with video and photographs of the Lamas and digitizing ARCHIVE materials.

Dissemination involves making the Lamas' teachings available through various avenues including books for free distribution and sale, lightly edited transcripts, a monthly e-letter (see below), DVDs, articles in *Mandala* and other magazines and on our website. Irrespective of the medium we choose, the teachings require a significant amount of work to prepare them for distribution.

This is just a summary of what we do. The ARCHIVE was established with virtually no seed funding and has developed solely through the kindness of many people, some of whom we have mentioned at the front of this book and most of the others on our website. We sincerely thank them all.

Our further development similarly depends upon the generosity of those who see the benefit and necessity of this work, and we would be extremely grateful for your help. Thus we hereby appeal to you for your kind support. If you would like to make a contribution to help us with any of the above tasks or to sponsor books for free distribution, please contact us:

LAMA YESHE WISDOM ARCHIVE
PO Box 636, Lincoln, MA 01773, USA
Telephone (781) 259-4466; Fax (678) 868-4806
info@LamaYeshe.com
www.LamaYeshe.com

The LAMA YESHE WISDOM ARCHIVE is a 501(c)(3) tax-deductible, non-profit corporation dedicated to the welfare of all sentient beings and totally dependent upon your donations for its continued existence. Thank you so much for your support. You may contribute by mailing a check, bank draft or money order to our Lincoln address; by making a donation on our secure website; by mailing us your credit card number or phoning it in; or by transferring funds directly to our bank—ask us for details.

LAMA YESHE WISDOM ARCHIVE MEMBERSHIP

In order to raise the money we need to employ editors to make available the thousands of hours of teachings mentioned above, we have established a membership plan. Membership costs US$1,000 and its main benefit is that you will be helping make the Lamas' incredible teachings available to a worldwide audience. More direct and tangible benefits to you personally include free Lama Yeshe and Lama Zopa Rinpoche books from the ARCHIVE and Wisdom Publications, a year's subscription to *Mandala*, a year of monthly pujas by the monks and nuns at Kopan Monastery with your personal dedication, and access to an exclusive members-only section of our website containing special, unpublished teachings currently unavailable to others. Please see www.LamaYeshe.com for more information.

MONTHLY E-LETTER

Each month we send out a free e-letter containing our latest news and a previously unpublished teaching by Lama Yeshe or Lama Zopa Rinpoche. To see nearly eighty back-issues or to subscribe with your email address, please go to our website.

THE FOUNDATION FOR THE PRESERVATION OF THE MAHAYANA TRADITION

The Foundation for the Preservation of the Mahayana Tradition (FPMT) is an international organization of Buddhist meditation study and retreat centers, both urban and rural, monasteries, publishing houses, healing centers and other related activities founded in 1975 by Lama Thubten Yeshe and Lama Thubten Zopa Rinpoche. At present, there are more than 160 FPMT centers and related activities in over thirty countries worldwide.

The FPMT has been established to facilitate the study and practice of Mahayana Buddhism in general and the Tibetan Gelug tradition, founded in the fifteenth century by the great scholar, yogi and saint, Lama Je Tsongkhapa, in particular.

Every quarter, the Foundation publishes a wonderful news journal, *Mandala*, from its International Office in the United States of America. To subscribe or view back issues, please go to the *Mandala* website, www.mandalamagazine.org, or contact:

FPMT
1632 SE 11th Avenue, Portland, OR 97214
Telephone (503) 808-1588; Fax (503) 808-1589
info@fpmt.org
www.fpmt.org

The FPMT website also offers teachings by His Holiness the Dalai Lama, Lama Yeshe, Lama Zopa Rinpoche and many other highly respected teachers in the tradition, details about the FPMT's educational programs, audio through FPMT radio, a complete listing of FPMT centers all over the world and in your area, a link to the excellent FPMT Store, and links to FPMT centers on the web, where you will find details of their programs, and to other interesting Buddhist and Tibetan home pages.

DISCOVERING BUDDHISM AT HOME OR ONLINE

Awakening the limitless potential of your mind,
achieving all peace and happiness

Over 2500 years ago, Shakyamuni Buddha gained direct insight into the nature of reality, perfected the qualities of wisdom, compassion, and power, and revealed the path to his disciples. In the 11th Century, Atisha brought these teachings to Tibet in the form of the lam-rim—the stages on the path to enlightenment. The lam-rim tradition found its pinnacle in the teachings of the great Tibetan saint Je Tsongkhapa in the 14th Century, and these teachings continued to pass from teacher to student up to this present day.

When Lama Thubten Yeshe and Lama Zopa Rinpoche transmitted these teachings to their disciples, they imparted a deeply experiential tradition of study and practice, leading thousands of seekers to discover the truth of what the Buddha taught. This tradition is the core of *Discovering Buddhism*—a two-year, fourteen-module series that provides a solid foundation in the teachings and practice of Tibetan Mahayana Buddhism.

HOW IT WORKS: Each *Discovering Buddhism* module consists of teachings, meditations and practices, readings, assessment questions, and a short retreat. Students who complete all the components of each course receive a completion card. When all fourteen modules have been completed, students receive a certificate of completion, a symbol of commitment to spiritual awakening.

This program is offered in FPMT centers around the world, as a home study program and now as an interactive online program as well.

Each module of both the home study and online program contains audio recordings of teachings and meditations given by qualified Western teachers, course materials and transcripts, online discussion forum overseen by senior FPMT teachers and completion certificates. FAQ pages help the student navigate the program and provide the best of the discussion board's questions and answers. Upon completion of a module, students may have their assessment questions evaluated by senior FPMT teachers and receive personal feedback.

Both *Discovering Buddhism at Home* and *Discovering Buddhism Online* are available from the FPMT Foundation Store, www.fpmt.org/shop or by becoming a Friend of FPMT, www.fpmt.org/friends. For more information on *Discovering Buddhism* and the other educational programs and services of the FPMT, please visit us at www.fpmt.org/education.

Other teachings of Lama Yeshe and Lama Zopa Rinpoche currently available

Books published by Wisdom Publications
Wisdom Energy, by Lama Yeshe and Lama Zopa Rinpoche
Introduction to Tantra, by Lama Yeshe
Transforming Problems, by Lama Zopa Rinpoche
The Door to Satisfaction, by Lama Zopa Rinpoche
Becoming Vajrasattva: The Tantric Path of Purification, by Lama Yeshe
The Bliss of Inner Fire, by Lama Yeshe
Becoming the Compassion Buddha, by Lama Yeshe
Ultimate Healing, by Lama Zopa Rinpoche
Dear Lama Zopa, by Lama Zopa Rinpoche
How to Be Happy, by Lama Zopa Rinpoche
Wholesome Fear, by Lama Zopa Rinpoche with Kathleen McDonald

About Lama Yeshe:
Reincarnation: The Boy Lama, by Vicki Mackenzie

About Lama Zopa Rinpoche:
The Lawudo Lama, by Jamyang Wangmo

You can get more information about and order the above titles at www.wisdompubs.org or call toll free in the USA on 1-800-272-4050.

Transcripts, practices and other materials
See the LYWA and FPMT websites for transcripts of teachings by Lama Yeshe and Lama Zopa Rinpoche and other practices written or compiled by Lama Zopa Rinpoche.

DVDs of Lama Yeshe
We are in the process of converting our VHS videos of Lama Yeshe's teachings to DVD. *The Three Principal Aspects of the Path*, *Introduction to Tantra*, *Offering Tsok to Heruka Vajrasattva*, *Anxiety in the Nuclear Age*, *Bringing Dharma to the West* and *Lama Yeshe at Disneyland* are currently available. More coming all the time—see our website for details.

DVDs of Lama Zopa Rinpoche
There are many available: see the Store on the FPMT website for more information.

What to do with Dharma teachings

The Buddhadharma is the true source of happiness for all sentient beings. Books like this show you how to put the teachings into practice and integrate them into your life, whereby you get the happiness you seek. Therefore, anything containing Dharma teachings, the names of your teachers or holy images is more precious than other material objects and should be treated with respect. To avoid creating the karma of not meeting the Dharma again in future lives, please do not put books (or other holy objects) on the floor or underneath other stuff, step over or sit upon them, or use them for mundane purposes such as propping up wobbly tables. They should be kept in a clean, high place, separate from worldly writings, and wrapped in cloth when being carried around. These are but a few considerations.

Should you need to get rid of Dharma materials, they should not be thrown in the rubbish but burned in a special way. Briefly: do not incinerate such materials with other trash, but alone, and as they burn, recite the mantra OM AH HUM. As the smoke rises, visualize that it pervades all of space, carrying the essence of the Dharma to all sentient beings in the six samsaric realms, purifying their minds, alleviating their suffering, and bringing them all happiness, up to and including enlightenment. Some people might find this practice a bit unusual, but it is given according to tradition. Thank you very much.

Dedication

Through the merit created by preparing, reading, thinking about and sharing this book with others, may all teachers of the Dharma live long and healthy lives, may the Dharma spread throughout the infinite reaches of space, and may all sentient beings quickly attain enlightenment.

In whichever realm, country, area or place this book may be, may there be no war, drought, famine, disease, injury, disharmony or unhappiness, may there be only great prosperity, may everything needed be easily obtained, and may all be guided by only perfectly qualified Dharma teachers, enjoy the happiness of Dharma, have love and compassion for all sentient beings, and only benefit and never harm each other.

LAMA THUBTEN YESHE was born in Tibet in 1935. At the age of six, he entered the great Sera Monastic University, Lhasa, where he studied until 1959, when the Chinese invasion of Tibet forced him into exile in India. Lama Yeshe continued to study and meditate in India until 1967, when, with his chief disciple, Lama Thubten Zopa Rinpoche, he went to Nepal. Two years later he established Kopan Monastery, near Kathmandu, in order to teach Buddhism to Westerners. In 1974, the Lamas began making annual teaching tours to the West, and as a result of these travels a worldwide network of Buddhist teaching and meditation centers—the Foundation for the Preservation of the Mahayana Tradition (FPMT)—began to develop. In 1984, after an intense decade of imparting a wide variety of incredible teachings and establishing one FPMT activity after another, at the age of forty-nine, Lama Yeshe passed away. He was reborn as Ösel Hita Torres in Spain in 1985 and recognized as the incarnation of Lama Yeshe by His Holiness the Dalai Lama in 1986. Lama's remarkable story is told in Vicki Mackenzie's book, *Reincarnation: The Boy Lama* (Wisdom Publications, 1996) and Adele Hulse's official biography, *Big Love,* (forthcoming from LYWA).

DR. NICHOLAS RIBUSH, MB, BS, is a graduate of Melbourne University Medical School (1964) who first encountered Buddhism at Kopan Monastery, Nepal, in 1972. Since then he has been a student of Lama Yeshe and Lama Zopa Rinpoche and a full time worker for their international organization, the Foundation for the Preservation of the Mahayana Tradition (FPMT). He was a monk from 1974 to 1986. He established FPMT archiving and publishing activities at Kopan in 1973 and with Lama Yeshe founded Wisdom Publications in 1975. Between 1981 and 1996 he served variously as Wisdom's director, editorial director and director of development. Over the years he has edited and published many teachings by His Holiness the Dalai Lama, Lama Yeshe, Lama Zopa Rinpoche and many other teachers and established and/or directed several other FPMT activities, including the International Mahayana Institute, Tushita Mahayana Meditation Centre, the Enlightened Experience Celebration, Mahayana Publications, Kurukulla Center for Tibetan Buddhist Studies and now the LAMA YESHE WISDOM ARCHIVE. He was a member of the FPMT board of directors from its inception in 1983 until 2002 and currently serves on the boards of LYWA, Kurukulla Center and Maitripa College.